The *Secretary* in
Training

A Practical Workbook for

Office Organisation and Secretarial Procedures

• Shirley Taylor •

Longman Singapore Publishers (Pte) Limited
25, First Lok Yang Road, Singapore 629734

*Associated companies, branches and
representatives throughout the world*

© Shirley Taylor

First published 1996

ISBN 981 223 310 5

Produced by Longman Singapore Publishers (Pte) Limited
Printed in Singapore

Designed by   Eddy Cheong
              Lynnica Lee
Edited by   Ang Chieh Ying

CONTENTS

PART 2: SECRETARIAL PROCEDURES

Unit 5 Organisational Skills

Unit 6 The Secretary in Practice

APPENDIX

Examination Papers

INDEX

INTRODUCTION

The Secretary in Training – A Practical Workbook for Office Organisation and Secretarial Procedures contains a series of worksheets which are designed to be user-friendly for both students and teachers.

There are many textbooks covering the theory of office practice and secretarial duties which provide essential information for anyone preparing to work in a clerical or secretarial capacity. However, the speed of technological development means it would be impossible for any one textbook to provide completely up-to-date information.

Using this *Workbook* does not mean that reference to such traditional textbooks will not be necessary. On the contrary, you are encouraged to do background reading and undertake further research. This is particularly important where certain aspects of some topics are unique in different parts of the world and also in topics which are subject to continual change.

Unlike traditional textbooks, this *Workbook* is designed to help you to help yourself. In particular I hope the practical nature of this *Workbook* will:

1   encourage you to think for yourself and apply information which you may already know

2   stimulate a desire to want to learn things for yourself and encourage you to do background reading and undertake further research where necessary

3   supplement your teacher's interpretation of the subject if used in a traditional classroom environment

ORGANISATION

The units are flexibly organised and self-contained so that an appropriate learning sequence can be arranged according to the syllabus and level being studied. Each unit contains a series of worksheets which take you through topics logically. They may be worked alone or with teacher-guided instruction. Worksheets feature gapfills to encourage thought and questions to stimulate discussion. **Check it out!** is a special feature designed to encourage further research or project work. At the end of each unit see how much you can remember in the **Quick Quiz**, and test your understanding in more detail in the **Review** section which features examination-style questions.

For those of you aiming to take specific written examinations, the **Appendix** contains several complete examination papers from **Pitman Qualifications** and the **LCCI Examinations Board**.

FILE-KEEPING

If you intend to be an efficient secretary you should start out in the right way by being organised in your studies. As you progress through the course, a loose-leaf ring binder with dividers labelled according to each unit in this *Workbook* will be useful. As discussions are stimulated by the text, write up separate notes to keep in your files. Together with your *Workbook*, these additional notes will be useful for reference in pre-examination revision.

AIMS

This *Workbook* should prove useful to anyone training to enter an office in a clerical, administrative or secretarial capacity. It will be particularly appropriate to students studying for a wide range of qualifications from any of the major examining bodies.

I hope you enjoy using **The Secretary in Training – A Practical Workbook for Office Organisation and Secretarial Procedures.**

Best wishes for success in your examinations and in your chosen career.

Shirley Taylor

Note: In order to retain consistency and fluency of text, a secretary has been referred to as 'she' and 'Chairman' used instead of 'Chairperson'. This is simply for convenience and no discrimination of the sexes is intended.

ACKNOWLEDGEMENTS

I am very grateful to The London Chamber of Commerce and Industry Examinations Board and Pitman Qualifications for giving permission to reproduce some past examination papers.

Serveral people have contributed in different ways to the successful completion of this project and I send sincere thanks to them all.

Once again to David Buckland for your confidence in this project, also to Leslie Lim and the rest of your team for continuing support.

To my editor, Chieh Ying, and the talented designers and artists, Eddy Cheong, Lynnica Lee and Alison Goh, for making such a valuable contribution with your hard work, innovation and creative flair.

To Douglas for use of your guest room on my visits to Singapore, and to Aida for looking after me so well during those visits.

Special thanks to Pam Forrester for always being there with constant encouragement and a friendship which I value dearly.

Last but by no means least, a big thank you to my Mum, the best secretary and the biggest supporter I could ever have.

Shirley Taylor

Part 1:

Office
Organisation

The Office World

WHAT IS AN OFFICE?

Everyone has their own idea of what they think of as 'an office'. One person may visualise a huge towering building containing hundreds of employees, supervisors and executives. To someone else an office may be a small room staffed by one person responsible to one or two managers. There could be as many different images of an office as there are students in your class. However, regardless of the environment itself, any office will carry out similar activities.

So what exactly is an office? Simply, an office is any place where clerical workers deal with *information*. This flowchart shows what happens to information in an office.

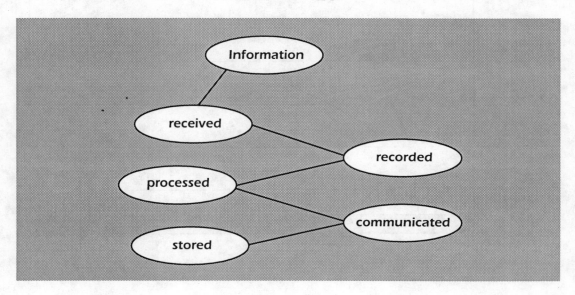

The type of information processed and the methods used will depend on various factors. Write them in the blanks below.

1 The _____ of   2 The _____ of

   the company.   the company's business.

Although the work performed varies according to the type of office, a lot of routine clerical work happens in most organisations. Can you add some more items to this list?

- receiving and routing telephone calls

- dealing with visitors

- _____

- _____

- _____

- _____

- _____

- _____

- _____

Business Organisations

There are many different types of business organisation which fall under the general headings of profit or non-profit making organisations. The following illustration shows the general structure of each category.

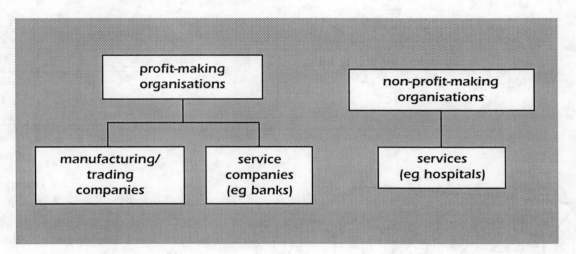

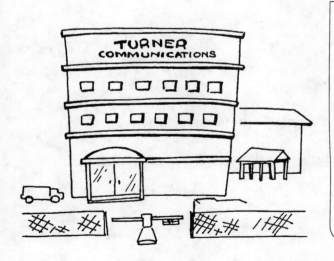

Check it out! Discuss the types of business organisations which exist in your own locality and make a list under each of the above headings. Make notes for your file.

Office Location and Design

The location of offices is a very important issue. Can you think of some factors which companies would consider when choosing a suitable site?

1 _____

2 _____

3 _____

Internal design of offices is equally important, especially to employees. There are three main types of office layout, cellular, open plan and landscaped offices. Insert the appropriate name in the following descriptions.

1 _____ are traditional, square or rectangular offices, with doors and (if you're lucky) windows.

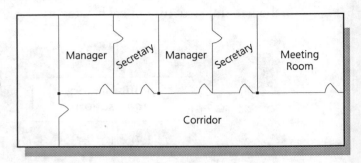

2 _____ are becoming very common in larger companies. Large spaces are sectioned off with potted plants and screens, and several levels of office staff work in the various sections, from office juniors to executives.

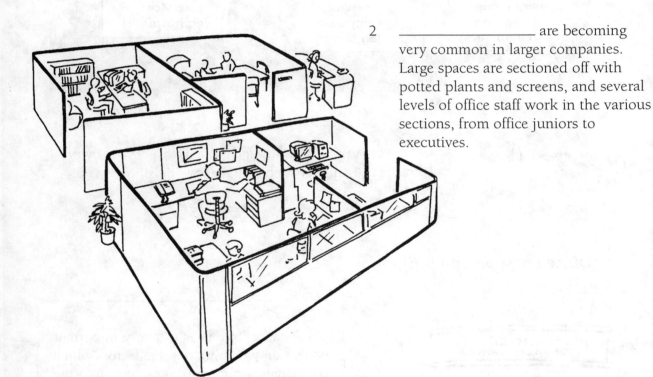

3 When open plan offices take on very large proportions, maybe

accommodating hundreds of staff, these are known as _____.

In which type of office would you like to work? Before you decide, consider the advantages and disadvantages of working in cellular and open plan offices. In this case, some advantages on one side turn into disadvantages on the other. See if you can complete this list and perhaps add to it with more reasons of your own.

Traditional Cellular Office

Advantages

1 Offices are lockable, providing privacy.

2 _____

   _____

3 You can control your own lighting/ heating/air conditioning.

4 _____

   _____

5 The environment can be made very personal to suit you.

Disadvantages

1 _____

   _____

2 Flow of work will be slower, going from office to office.

3 _____

   _____

Open Plan Office

Disadvantages

1 _____

   _____

2 If you need to concentrate, it could be noisy.

3 _____

   _____

4 Security is reduced as there are no doors to lock.

5 _____

   _____

Advantages

1 With all staff on view supervision is easier.

2 _____

   _____

3 More economical use of space/utilities, so cheaper to maintain.

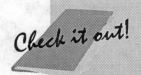

Office furniture is also very important to employees. Well-designed furniture can ensure good health and efficiency. Collect some leaflets from your local furniture stores and design your ideal working environment. Make a poster for your classroom wall.

The Secretary's Role in Large and Small Offices

Apart from the physical size of the office, there are advantages to be gained from working in both small and large organisations. However, when choosing a working environment some considerations would be more important to one person than to another.

Find out whether you are better suited to working in a small office or a large one by choosing *a* or *b* in the following statements.

I would prefer to work in an environment where

1. a The organisational structure is clearly laid down. It will not worry me that I may have no involvement with some departments or employees.

   b Everyone knows everyone else and the working environment feels rather like a family.

2. a I can specialise in one area of work and become expert.
   b I can have a large variety of different types of work.

3. a There are clearly laid down rules and procedures, company handbooks and official contracts, so that everyone knows what is expected of them.

   b There are no set rules and regulations. The atmophere is more informal and I can help to set the standards.

4. a There are good welfare facilities like sports clubs and social clubs, canteen facilities.

   b There are no organised welfare facilities so I choose my own recreation outside work.

5   a   There are active staff development and training programmes, perhaps day release to local colleges to further my qualifications.

       b   There are no formal training programmes.

6   a   Salary scales are laid down, with criteria like age, length of service, position, etc.

       b   There are no set scales but workers are rewarded by management accordingly.

7   a   More jobs are available so there are better chances for promotion.

       b   Variety and flexibility are more important than advancement.

8   a   Equipment is modern and up-to-date.

       b   I do not have to learn how to use new machinery all the time.

If you ticked more *a* statements, then working in a large organisation is definitely for you. If you ticked more *b* statements, then perhaps you are more suited to working in a small company.

1.2 INTERNAL ORGANISATION

When a business starts to grow, employees normally specialise in different aspects of the work. Separate departments will be created with a manager in charge of each one. In this illustration of an organisation chart the first initial of some key departments of a typical company have been provided. Insert the department names.

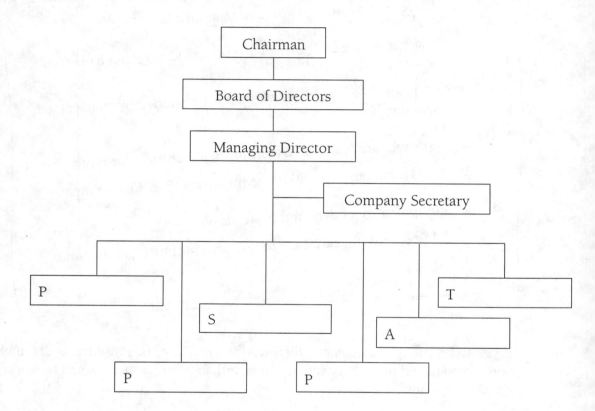

Check it out! Discuss in your class or in groups the responsibilities of the senior executives at the head of this organisation chart and the key functions of each of these departments. Make notes to keep in your file.

Centralisation of Office Services

Some companies prefer that all activities of each department are contained within individual departments. In this decentralised system each department will have its own specialised staff, filing and copying facilities, etc.

Many large firms now use a centralised system, where some office services are shared by all departments. These commonly-used office services will be centralised in one location. In the boxes below, write down the names of some services which might be centralised.

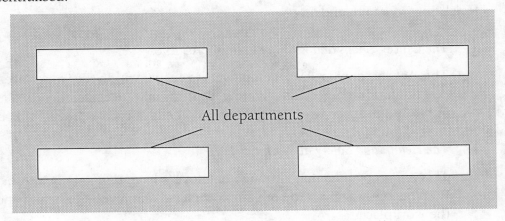

All departments

Here is a checklist showing the advantages of centralisation. Discuss the disadvantages and complete this checklist too.

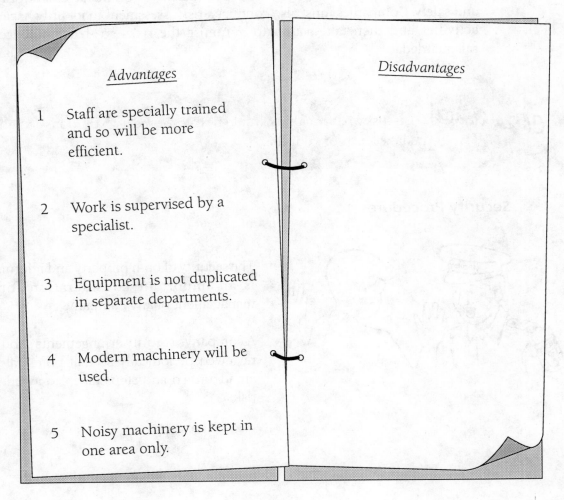

Advantages

1   Staff are specially trained and so will be more efficient.

2   Work is supervised by a specialist.

3   Equipment is not duplicated in separate departments.

4   Modern machinery will be used.

5   Noisy machinery is kept in one area only.

Disadvantages

Safety and Security in the Office

An essential concern of any company should be to provide a safe and comfortable working environment for its employees. In the UK there are three acts covering legislation on health and safety.

- *The Offices, Shops and Railway Premises Act 1963*

  This Act lays down rules for employers to ensure within the workplace minimum conditions for temperature, lighting, washing and toilet facilities, first aid, as well as minimum space which should be provided for each worker (400 cubic feet).

- *The Health and Safety at Work Act 1974*

  This Act recognises that although employees have rights, they also have duties. Responsibility is given to both employers and employees for health and safety in the workplace.

- *Health and Safety at Work (Management) Regulations 1992*

  This Act requires companies with more than five employees to appoint a competent person (eg a Safety Representative) to provide advice on management of health and safety. Companies must also conduct a risk assessment to identify hazardous activities and then take action to minimise the risks so that employees are safeguarded.

Check it out! Discuss what you think would be categorised as 'hazardous activities'. Make a list for your file.

Security Procedures

The security of both property and information is an important consideration for the management of any company.

A company's security arrangements should be reviewed periodically so that potential risks are identified and steps taken to avoid such risks.

Thieves realise the potential of not only expensive equipment but also information which could prove valuable. What type of information do you think would be valuable to thieves? Make notes for your file.

1 _____   4 _____

2 _____   5 _____

3 _____   6 _____

Check it out! Discuss security procedures which an organisation could take to protect itself. Make notes for your file.

Fire Prevention

Organisations take various steps to endeavour to prevent or reduce the risks of fire in their offices. Use words from the box to complete the sentences below.

evacuation   escapes   extinguishers   alarm system

regulations   flammable   blocked

1   Always comply with fire department _____.

2   Areas where _____ materials are stored should be designated 'No Smoking'.

3   In case of fire, all fire _____ should be clearly signposted.

4   Fire escapes should never be _____ by boxes or other objects.

5   Fire drills should be held and the _____ tested regularly.

6   Notices regarding _____ procedures in the event of a fire should be clearly displayed.

7   Staff should be trained in the use of fire _____ and hoses which should be located at various points around the offices and checked regularly.

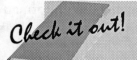

What legislation exists in your country in regard to health and safety?

The Office World

Circle your answers or write them in the space provided.

1   The Chief Executive in any organisation is usually
  a   the Company Secretary.
  b   the Chairman.
  c   the Managing Director.
  d   the Financial Director.

2   An organisation chart shows
  a   the flow of information in a business.
  b   the work carried out by employees.
  c   departments and key personnel in a company.
  d   the location of different departments.

3   The Production Department would deal with
  a   company legal obligations.
  b   wages and salaries.
  c   inspection and quality control.
  d   market research.

4   The Marketing Department would deal with
  a   employee services.
  b   market research.
  c   production planning.
  d   office services.

5   The Personnel Department would deal with
  a   purchasing and stores.
  b   training.
  c   advertising.
  d   stock control.

6   A company's Board of Directors are chosen by the

    a   employees.

    b   shareholders.

    c   senior managers.

    d   Chairman.

7   A key advantage of working in a small company is that

    a   you will not have much work to do.

    b   you will have more variety and responsibility.

    c   you can negotiate your own salary.

    d   you can make tea whenever you like.

8   Which type of office layout would make more economical use of space, lighting and temperature control?

    a   A cellular office

    b   An open planned office

    c   The Chairman's office

9   Who or what department would be responsible for the following:

    a   Reporting to the Board of Directors on the day-to-day operation of the business?

    _____

    b   Preparing reports for shareholders and the board of directors?

    _____

    c   Carrying out research into potential demand for a new product?

    _____

    d   Receiving payments from debtors and paying bills from creditors?

    _____

10   *The Health and Safety at Work Act* identifies the duties of employers, managers and individual workers in relation to health and safety. Suggest one precaution you can take at the end of each day.

_____

_____

Review

1   a   What are the main features of open plan offices?
     b   Suggest three advantages of open plan offices to both management
          and staff.

2   If someone injures themselves in your office, list the procedures which
     should be followed.

Communications

The Reception Area

The reception area will normally be situated at the main entrance of a building or suite of offices. It should be clearly indicated from the outside, tidy, attractive and welcoming on the inside.

Apart from the basic office furniture, an efficient reception area would contain many other items. Can you add some items to this list to make a reception area more efficient and attractive?

1. Coat stand
2. Clock
3. Chairs/coffee tables
4. Reading material
5. _____
6. _____
7. _____
8. _____
9. _____
10. _____

The Receptionist

First impressions are vital. Acting as a link between the public and the organisation, the receptionist plays a key role.

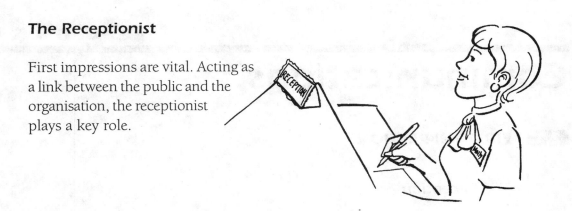

Can you rearrange these letters to make some words which describe the qualities a good receptionist should possess?

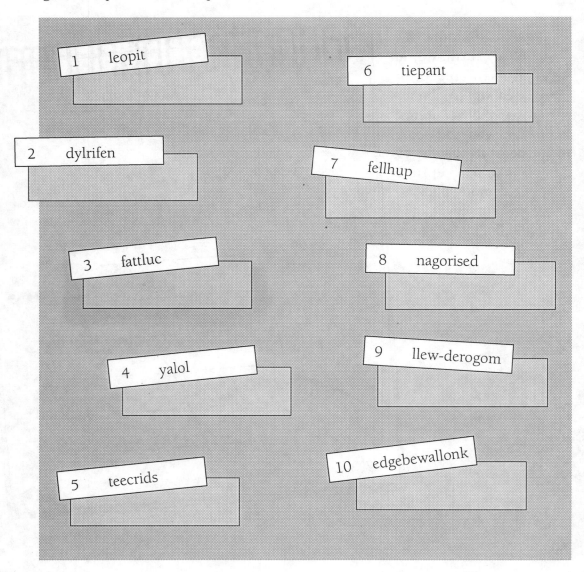

1   leopit

2   dylrifen

3   fattluc

4   yalol

5   teecrids

6   tiepant

7   fellhup

8   nagorised

9   llew-derogom

10   edgebewallonk

Dealing with Visitors

Discuss the procedure for dealing with visitors by completing this flowchart.

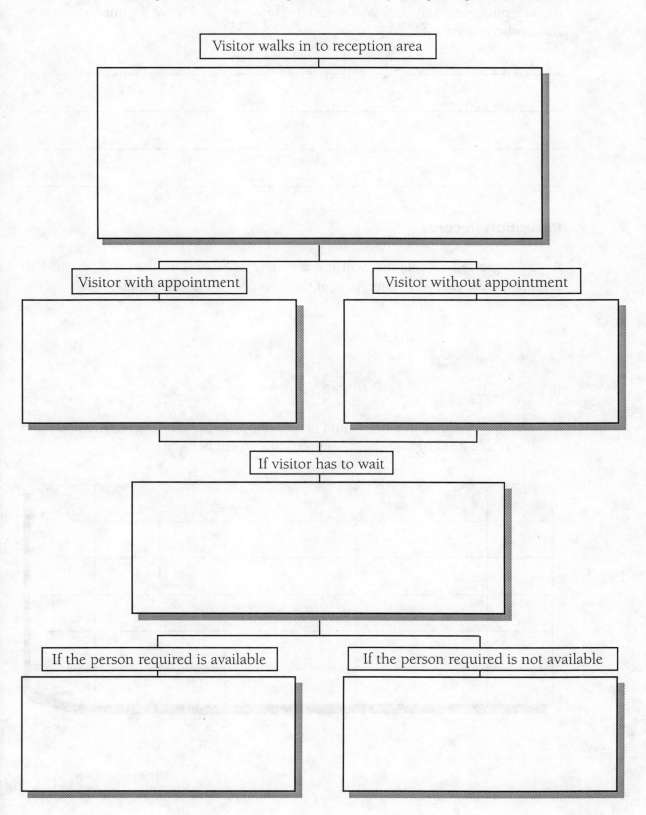

Visitor walks in to reception area

Visitor with appointment

Visitor without appointment

If visitor has to wait

If the person required is available

If the person required is not available

Other Duties of the Receptionist

The main job of the receptionist is to look after visitors to the company and to keep the reception area tidy and well-stocked. However, there may be time to perform some other duties, such as:

_____

_____

_____

_____

Reception Records

A well-organised receptionist will use a variety of records to maintain an efficient reception area. Can you name some of these records from their descriptions?

1 _____ of Callers

All callers to a company should be asked to 'sign in'. Can you suggest and fill in suitable headings for the columns of this record book?

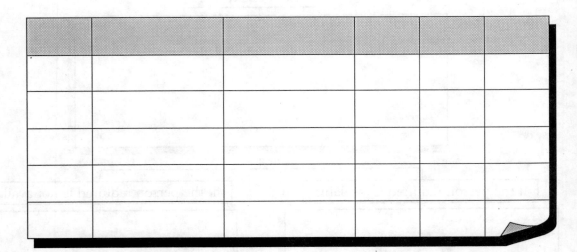

2 _____ Book

A receptionist may use one of these to make a note of visitors who are expected each day.

3 Staff _____

A receptionist may find it useful to record the movement of the key personnel who are frequently in and out of the office. This would also include staff on holiday or away on sick leave.

4 _____ Index

Most visitors will leave their calling card with the receptionist. They should be kept in an A-Z index under the name of the company - never under the name of the person, as this may change.

5 _____ List

The receptionist will need an up-to-date list of all employees and their telephone extension numbers.

Check it out!

Larger organisations have standard procedures for dealing with visitors and maintaining security. Discuss these procedures and make notes for your file.

Quick Quiz

Reception

A   *Choose suitable words to complete the following sentences.*

1   As the first person a visitor meets in a company, the receptionist should give a good _____.

2   The receptionist should be very knowledgeable about the company's _____.

3   A _____ should be kept to record details of all visitors, their arrival time and person visited.

4   It is good practice to ask for caller's _____ and to file these for future reference.

5   A reception area must be kept tidy and _____.

B   *Choose the correct answer from the choices given.*

1   A receptionist should have a name plate on the desk or uniform because
   a   visitors can ask the receptionist for a date.
   b   visitors prefer to address the receptionist by name.
   c   it makes the atmosphere more informal.

2   When a visitor expresses appreciation, the receptionist should respond by saying
   a   "Any time dear. Don't mention it!"
   b   "You're very welcome."
   c   "No problem. Just bring flowers next time eh?!"

3   For security purposes many organisations require visitors to wear a special
   a   uniform.
   b   visitor's badge.
   c   arm band.

4   Departments often accessed by visitors (like Personnel, Sales and Purchasing) will normally be situated
   a   on the top floor of the building.
   b   as close to reception as possible.
   c   near the canteen.

5   If a visitor has to wait for a while in reception, the receptionist should
   a   chat on the phone with a colleague and exchange company gossip.
   b   offer the visitor refreshments/reading material.
   c   chat to the visitor constantly to make sure he does not feel lonely.

Review

1   Make a list of the main differences in the duties of a receptionist in small and large organisations.

2   Your company has introduced uniforms for its two receptionists. What benefits would be gained by the company?

All companies rely on the telephone as an important method of communication, both internally and externally, and most employees will have access to a telephone. It is vital to develop a good telephone technique.

The following is a verbatim telephone conversation between a potential customer and a new telephonist at Turner Communications. Choose players to act out the conversation.

(*The phone rings*)

Telephonist	Hello?
Caller	Hello? Is that Turner Communications?
Telephonist	Yes it is.
Caller	Can I speak to Mr Turner please?
Telephonist	You just missed him. He went out.
Caller	Oh dear, and it is rather important. When will he be back in the office?
Telephonist	Can't say. He doesn't tell me anything.
Caller	Hmmm … Can I speak to his secretary then?
Telephonist	Hang on, I'll see if she's free … No, her line's busy. You're not having much luck, are you?
Caller	(*Sighing*) Well perhaps there's someone else who could help me regarding settlement of our account. I …
Telephonist	(*Interrupting*) Can't you ring back later?
Caller	No I cannot. Perhaps Mr Turner or his secretary could call me? My name is Mr Foster.
Telephonist	OK but I'm not sure when they'll be able to call you.
Caller	Please just pass on the message that I would like my call returned as soon as possible. My …
Telephonist	OK I'll do that, no problem.
Caller	(*Sarcastically*) Would you like my telephone number?
Telephonist	(*Giggling*) Oh yeah, that would help wouldn't it?!
Caller	It's 4582783.
Telephonist	Hang on while I get a pen. (*She fumbles in a desk for a pen and paper.*) OK, fire away.
Caller	4582783.
Telephonist	Got it! Thanks then. Bye for now. (*She hangs up. The caller stares at the disconnected phone in his hand and sighs heavily.*)

What was wrong?

1   What should the telephonist have said when she picked up the telephone?

    _____

2   Suggest what the telephonist could have said instead of "You just missed him. He went out."

    _____

3   Which department could the caller have been referred to?

    _____

4   What should be by the side of every telephone?

    a   _____

    b   _____

    c   _____

5   Suggest more suitable expressions instead of

    a   "OK but I'm not sure when they'll be able to call you."

        _____

    b   "OK I'll do that, no problem."

        _____

    c   "Got it!"

        _____

6   Suggest two other details the telephonist should have obtained from the caller.

    a   _____

    b   _____

25

7 With which hand should the telephonist pick up the telephone handset?

_____

8 If you were cut off in the middle of a telephone conversation, what would you do?
   a   Call the other person back immediately.
   b   Wait for the other person to call you back.

9 If an internal call was coming through at the same time as an external call, which would you deal first?

_____

10 How can you make sure you always sound pleasant on the telephone?

_____

Telephone Messages

By the side of every telephone, whether internal or external, there should be a note pad and pen or pencil so that notes can be taken for passing on messages.

Suggest suitable headings for this blank telephone message form. Fill in your answers in the shaded portions.

MESSAGE FOR

While you were out

Telephone Alphabet

When you are required to spell out a word over the telephone you will normally use the telephone alphabet. The most common method now is to use country codes. For example, if you were spelling out the name Beijing, you would spell it:

Bangkok - England - India - Japan - India - Norway - Greece

Choose countries to complete the rest of the telephone alphabet.

A –		N –	Norway
B –	Bangkok	O –	
C –		P –	
D –		Q –	
E –	England	R –	
F –		S –	
G –	Greece	T –	
H –		U –	
I –	India	V –	
J –	Japan	W –	
K –		X –	
L –		Y –	
M –		Z –	

International Telephone Calls

Before making an international telephone call you must make special preparations. Complete the blanks in the checklist below.

1   Confirm the _____ and write it down.

2   Check the international dialling code as well as the _____

    code and the _____ code.

3   Check the _____ difference.

4   Consider if there is a _____ charge band.

5   Know the _____ of the person you need to speak to.

6   Prepare _____ on what you want to say.

7   Have any necessary _____ for reference.

8   Consider if you need any common _____ phrases.

9   Take special care when _____ the number.

10   Be prepared for overseas _____ to sound different.

Telephone Services

Each country's local telephone company provides many different services to telephone users. These differ from country to country, but some standard telephone services are described below. Can you choose the appropriate service from those in the following box?

Fixed Time Call	Person to Person Call	Alarm Call
Emergency Services	Advice of Duration and Charge	Phonecards
Transferred Charge Calls	Telephone Charge Card	Freefone
Information Services		

1   _____

If you have to catch an early plane or train, ask the operator to call you at a pre-arranged time.

2   _____

Using this service, you can pre-arrange for the required person to be by the telephone when you call. This is especially useful for overseas calls.

3 _____

This service will enable you to make a telephone call without paying any money. The operator will call the person required and ask if they are willing to pay for the call.

4 _____

Some companies use this service to encourage customers to call them, perhaps asking for product information to be sent to them. The cost of the call will be added to the account of the company.

5 _____

The user gives the operator a special number from a card as well as the telephone number required. The cost of the call goes to the relevant card account.

6 _____

This service is useful if making a call from someone else's line. The operator will tell you how long you were connected and how much the call will cost.

7 _____

Use this service to save time waiting to be connected to the person required. There is no charge for this call until the person required actually speaks on the telephone.

8 _____

These will avoid having to carry around coins for use in public telephones. Insert the card into the payphone and a display shows the amount left to spend.

9 _____

Many special pre-recorded messages are available, for instance the local weather forecast, the latest song, and even the horoscope for the day.

10 _____

In England it is 999. In America it is 911. Which number would you dial in your country when you need to report a fire, ask for an ambulance or call for the police?

Telecommunications develop so quickly. New products and services are being introduced constantly. In pairs or groups, choose one or more items from the following list and find out as much information as you can. Collect brochures and factsheets. Ask for extra information.

Present your findings as a formal report or a wall chart for display on your classroom wall. Perhaps an oral presentation could be made so that other members of your group can benefit too?

Choose topics from this list, but remember also to add any special services available in your own country.

- Developments in switchboards
- The latest telephones (including mobile phones)
- Telephone answering machines
- Paging systems
- Intercom/Public address systems
- Telegrams
- Telex
- Videotex
- Teleconferencing (including audioconferencing and video-conferencing)
- Fax

Telecommunications

A   Test your telephone technique.

1   *You are answering the telephone at Turner Communications. Write down what you would say in the following telephone conversation.*

2   *Draw up a telephone message form and fill in the appropriate message.*

You   _____

Caller   Good morning. Could I speak to Miss Turner please.

(Miss Turner is in a meeting and has asked not to be disturbed.)

You _____

Caller Oh dear. I need to speak to her rather urgently.

You _____

Caller No that's OK. Can you just pass on a message for Miss Turner to call me as soon as she is free?

You _____

Caller Yes, it's Mrs Martha Lim of Lim Technology.

You _____

Caller It's 4672312.

You _____

Caller Thank you very much. Goodbye.

You _____

B Circle your answers.

1. If you need to know the duration and cost of a telephone call made via the operator, you will ask for
   a a personal call.
   b an ADC call.
   c a fixed time call.

2 Alarm calls are offered by the telephone company
   a in case of burglary.
   b to warn callers who talk for too long.
   c to act as an early morning call.

3 Your company wishes to allow customers to call them without paying for the call. The best service to use is
   a a telephone charge card.
   b a transferred charge call.
   c freefone.

4   You want to call long distance at a time when you know the person required will be by the phone. Which service will you use?
    a   Person to person call
    b   Fixed time call
    c   Alarm call

5   You need to discuss an important issue with five colleagues, all of whom are situated at different locations in your country. There is no time to arrange a meeting but you want everyone to be involved in the discussion. Which service will you use?
    a   Transferred charge call
    b   Emergency Services
    c   Teleconference

C   *Name the telecommunication equipment or service which will be most suitable in the following circumstances.*

1   Your employer wants to contact you to ask you to come into his office for some dictation.

_____

2   Your employer is often away from the office and you need to maintain contact with him/her.

_____

3   You do not want to lose business when the office is closed.

_____

4   You need to send a message which will be received in all offices of the company simultaneously.

_____

5   You want to send a copy of a document to a colleague overseas because you need to discuss it with him before a meeting this afternoon.

_____

Review

1   Your company's telephone calls have been increasing recently and your employer asks you to suggest ways in which costs could be reduced.

2   Name three up-to-date methods of mobile communication and state their advantages.

2.3 BUSINESS TRANSACTIONS

Every time you enter a shop, you choose what you want to buy, pay for it and perhaps will be given a receipt. This type of business transaction is part of our everyday lives. Each time goods or services are sold, the trader makes a profit to cover things like rent, wages, lighting, utilities, etc.

The Buying and Selling Process

Large or small companies cannot just go shopping for things they need for their organisation. Many documents must pass between the buyer and the seller in any typical business transaction. In the illustration below, discuss the documents in the buying and selling process. The first one has been completed for you.

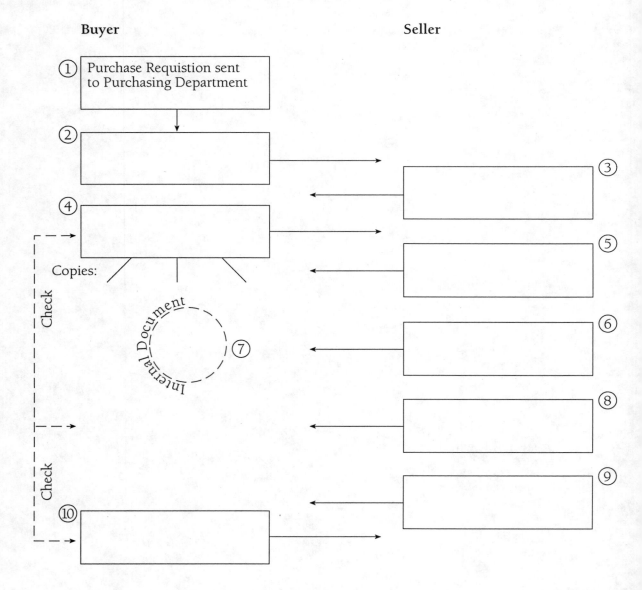

Purchase Requisition

Any employee makes out a purchase requisition when an item is required. This gives details of the item required

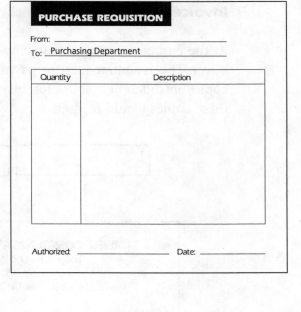

PURCHASE REQUISITION

From: _____

To: Purchasing Department _____

Quantity	Description

Authorized: _____   Date: _____

Quotation

After making telephone enquiries or sending out letters of enquiry, potential suppliers will forward quotations. The Purchasing Officer will make a choice based on price, availability, suitability and terms of payment.

TURNER COMMUNICATIONS plc
Lodge Lane Unit 141
Sheffield S31 0ES
Tel: 0114 2862131   Fax: 0114 2862214

To: Mr John Ang
Hillson Engineering Ltd
21 Farnham Grange
Sheffield
S20 2EX

Date: 15 March 1995

No: T29

QUOTATION

Dear Sir

Thank you for your recent enquiry. We have pleasure in quoting as follows

Qty	Description	Catalogue No	Price	VAT	Total
1	Fax Machine Pf 2001 EX	F291	405.00	70.88	475.88

Delivery: ex stock   Terms: 2.5% 30 days

I look forward to receiving your order.

Yours faithfully

E TURNER
Sales Manager

Purchase Order

An order will be based on the chosen quotation. It will have a special number and will be copied to the relevant departments. They are:

_____

_____

_____

ORDER **HILLSON ENGINEERING LTD**
21 Farnham Grange
Sheffield S20 2EX
Tel: 0114 462741
Fax: 0114 462681

Date 20 March 1995

To: Turner Communications plc
Lodge Lane
Unit 141
Sheffield
S31 0ES

No. T242

Please supply: .

Catalogue No.	Quantity	Description	£
F291	1	Fax Machine PF2001 EX	405.00
		VAT @ 17.5%	70.88
		Total	475.88

Terms 2.5% 30 days
Delivery Ex stock   Signature _____
Purchasing Officer

Invoice

At the end of the month following delivery, the seller would send an invoice to the buyer. This is a bill requesting payment. Invoice sets are normally printed with several copies in different colours for easy identification. Label this diagram to show how these copies would be used.

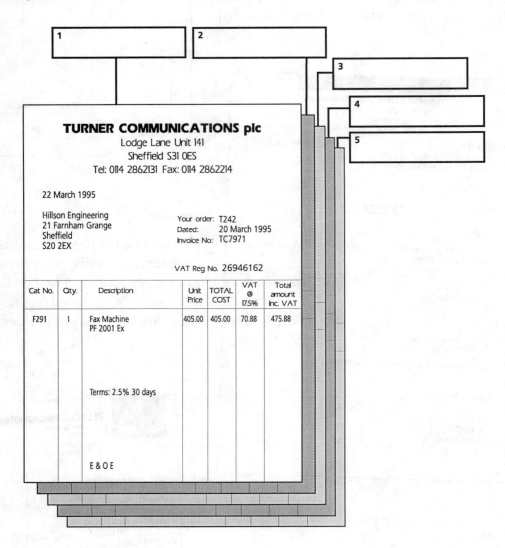

```
                                                    VAT Reg No. 26946162
```

TURNER COMMUNICATIONS plc
Lodge Lane Unit 141
Sheffield S31 0ES
Tel: 0114 2862131 Fax: 0114 2862214

22 March 1995

Hillson Engineering
21 Farnham Grange
Sheffield
S20 2EX

Your order: T242
Dated: 20 March 1995
Invoice No: TC7971

VAT Reg No. 26946162

Cat No.	Qty.	Description	Unit Price	TOTAL COST	VAT @ 17.5%	Total amount Inc. VAT
F291	1	Fax Machine PF 2001 Ex	405.00	405.00	70.88	475.88

Terms: 2.5% 30 days

E & O E

Debit Notes and Credit Notes

A *debit note* will be sent if a customer has been _____ on the invoice and actually owes the supplier *more* than the amount stated.

A *credit note* will be sent if a customer has been _____ on the invoice and owes the supplier *less* than the amount stated.

Statement

At the end of each month suppliers will send out statements to each customer. This shows every transaction which took place during the month, any payments made, any new purchases, and any credit or debit due.

TURNER COMMUNICATIONS plc
Lodge Lane Unit 141
Sheffield S31 0ES
Tel: 0114 2862131 Fax: 0114 2862214

STATEMENT

Hillson Engineering Ltd
21 Farnham Grange
Sheffield
S20 2EX

Statement Date: 30 March 1995

Date	Invoice No.	Purchases	Payments and Returns	Balance
1995		E		E
05 March				
22 March			285.00	----
	TC 7971	475.88		475.88
25 March	TC 7992	246.61		722.49

Terminology

The following terms are often used in business transactions. Make a note of these terms for your file, and write down their meanings for future reference.

Availability	Ex stock _____
	Ex works _____
Terms	Cash discount _____
	Trade discount _____
	Net monthly _____
	2.5% 30 days _____
Delivery	Carriage forward _____
	Carriage paid _____
VAT	_____
E&OE	_____
NCR	_____
Pro Forma Invoice	_____

Credit Control

Credit is normally used in business, with payment being made at the end of each month. However, precautions must be taken to prevent bad debts. Before granting credit to a new customer, references will normally be obtained from:

1 _____	or	2 _____

Delivery of goods will not be made until the references have been received. If goods are urgently required, however, there are two options for the new customer:

3 _____	or	4 _____

A *customer record card* will normally be made out so that a quick reference can be made to information about each customer. Examples of these record cards can be found in many reference books. Until the customer is very well-known a strict control of credit levels will usually be exercised.

If an account is *overdue*, it will be put on a _____.
Follow-up of overdue accounts is essential. If payment is not received after issuing the statement, the follow-up procedure may be:

1   Issue a _____.

2   Make a _____.

3   Send further _____ will be

4   When everything else has failed, _____
    taken by the company's solicitor.

Check it out!   Discuss with your classmates the procedures used in your company. Bring in some documents and forms to show your classmates. Could these be made into a wall chart?

Quick Quiz

Business Transactions

Circle your answers.

1 When you have completed a Purchase Requisition, to which department will you send it?
   a Sales Department
   b Purchasing Department
   c Accounts Department

2 Which department usually prepares invoices?
   a Sales Department
   b Purchasing Department
   c Accounts Department

3 Which department usually sends out statements?
   a Sales Department
   b Purchasing Department
   c Accounts Department

4 Cash discount is often offered to buyers to
   a encourage them to buy in bulk.
   b encourage them to pay promptly.
   c help them to make a profit.

5 When a quotation has been accepted, the Purchasing Department will send the supplier
   a a requisition note.
   b a delivery note.
   c an order.

6 Invoices usually show the expression E&OE. What does this mean?
   a Terms net monthly account
   b Goods are available in stock
   c Errors and omissions excepted

7 If a supplier has overcharged a customer on an invoice, what document would be issued?
   a A debit note
   b A credit note
   c A statement

39

8   A statement of account is sent out to all customers
a   at fixed intervals, usually monthly.
b   after each transaction.
c   once a year.

9   Ex stock means
a   the items required are not available.
b   items are available immediately.
c   stock will be received within 2 weeks.

10   Which of the following would be asked to provide a reference for a new customer?
a   The Managing Director
b   The company's solicitor
c   The company's banker

Review

1   Explain the difference between the following pairs of documents.

     a   Invoice and Debit Note
     b   Quotation and Estimate
     c   Catalogue and Price List
     d   Advice Note and Delivery Note

2   You work for the Administration Manager who is responsible for purchasing office equipment. List the main documents used in the purchasing procedure and give a brief explanation of each.

A tremendous amount of correspondence flows between organisations every day. Business often depends on being able to transmit information quickly and easily. Although modern technology now enables other means of communicating information, the traditional postal system is still widely used.

Postal Services

As a secretary your employer will expect you to be knowledgeable about all the services provided by the Post Office. Mail Room Clerks and Secretaries in the UK find the UK Post Office Guide a valuable source of information. Is there an equivalent guide in your own country?

Most post office services can be categorised under the following headings.

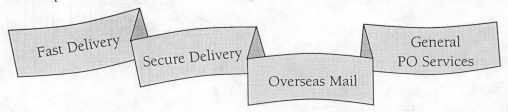

Fast Delivery   Secure Delivery   Overseas Mail   General PO Services

Find out about the following post office services (from discussion, from your textbooks or from the post office) and then decide in which category they belong. Make proper notes in your file, including brief descriptions of each item.

1 Special delivery	9 Express post
2 Freepost	10 Swiftair
3 Recorded delivery	11 Datapost
4 Cash on delivery service	12 Certificate of posting
5 Registered post	13 Redirection service
6 Business Reply Service	14 Poste restante
7 Private box numbers	15 Customs Declaration
8 Consequential Loss Insurance	

Check it out! The post office are constantly improving and increasing their services. Visit your local post office and collect some free leaflets regarding these services. You could make up a wall chart so that other students can benefit too.

Handling Mail

In the office you will be dealing with many different methods of communication, of which mail is just one. You will need to be aware of all the procedures used in your organisation so that you can deal with the mail for your boss efficiently.

The following scenario takes the mail from the mail room to the secretary and back again to the mail room. Complete the blanks.

1   Mail arrives in the company's mail room. Clerks will sort the mail in _____ and deliver to offices at regular intervals throughout each day.

2   Mail is delivered to the secretary's office. All mail will be opened except mail marked _____.

3   The secretary reads mail carefully and attaches the relevant _____ where necessary.

4 Mail is delivered to the employer. _____ may be given regarding any replies needed.

5 Correspondence is transcribed, and each item is kept in a

_____ .

At appropriate times during the day the secretary will obtain her employer's signature.

6 Envelopes for posting are placed in the secretary's 'Out' tray ready for collection by the

_____

at pre-arranged times.

7 Back in the Mail Room, mail is sorted, _____ and franked. Franked mail may be collected by the _____ .

Mail Room Machinery

Below are the descriptions of the types of equipment found in a mail room. Identify them and write your answers in the boxes.

1   This is useful for firms who send out a lot of mail regularly to the same people. Plates with names and addresses are prepared.

2   These are the latest weighing machines used for letters and parcels. Press the right keys and find out the weight and postage to anywhere in the world.

3   This machine will fold letters and other documents, and even put the documents into their envelopes.

4   This is used to destroy documents no longer needed, particularly confidential documents. Many companies recycle their waste paper.

5   This machine is useful when dealing with large volumes of paper. It sorts the documents according to the page order.

6   A sharp blade on this piece of equipment cuts off a tiny piece from the edge of envelopes.

7   This machine prints the value of postage on an envelope or label, together with the date/time, licence number and an advertising slogan.

The mail room would need other equipment and many sundry items for general daily use. How many can you think of?

1	_____	6	_____
2	_____	7	_____
3	_____	8	_____
4	_____	9	_____
5	_____	10	_____

Check it out! Individually or in pairs/groups, visit local equipment exhibitions or showrooms. Collect some leaflets on these items of equipment (and others). Make some posters for your classroom wall but present your findings to your class first.

Quick Quiz

Dealing with Mail

1 To which person or department would the Mail Room Clerk deliver the following mail?

a A credit note from a supplier _____

b A leaflet announcing a secretarial competition _____

c A request for a testimonial from a former employee _____

d An invoice from a supplier _____

e A telephone bill _____

f   Title deeds to a new warehouse   _____

g   Orders from a customer   _____

h   An insurance policy for company cars   _____

i   An office equipment brochure   _____

j   An enquiry about employment   _____

2   What services are being described in the following sentences?

a   The postman is paid for goods ordered from a mail order firm.

_____

b   Obtain one of these as proof that a letter has actually been posted.

_____

c   Use this service for sending important papers (eg a birth certificate) through the post.

_____

d   You can ensure that customers reply to your mailshots by using this service.

_____

e   Use this service to send valuable items through the post.

_____

f   When your office moves to a new location you will use this service so that mail is forwarded to your new address.

_____

Review

1 You are secretary to the Training Manager and the mail room clerk has delivered the following items today. How would you deal with each item?

    a   An envelope marked confidential.

    b   A letter complaining that the reply to a letter sent three weeks ago has not been received.

    c   A memo giving details of the next monthly Personnel and Training Department meeting.

    d   An invitation to a Training Exhibition to be held next month.

2 The Post Office now has a lot of competition from private delivery and courier services. Briefly explain the services they provide.

2.5 PROCESSING INFORMATION

Information processing is the term which describes the manipulation of information in words, numbers, images, graphics, even voice. The way information is processed in individual offices will depend on the size, complexity and the type of business concerned.

Technology used for processing information is constantly changing and the developments taking place constantly have exciting repercussions for all office workers. Before we look at the latest methods of processing information, let us first consider the general procedures and equipment with which a secretary must be familiar in order to process text.

Secretaries may receive work from their employers in a variety of different ways. Different employers may prefer to:

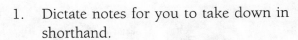

1. Dictate notes for you to take down in shorthand.

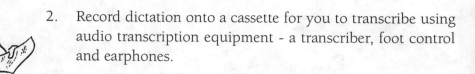

2. Record dictation onto a cassette for you to transcribe using audio transcription equipment - a transcriber, foot control and earphones.

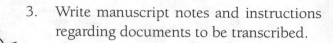

3. Write manuscript notes and instructions regarding documents to be transcribed.

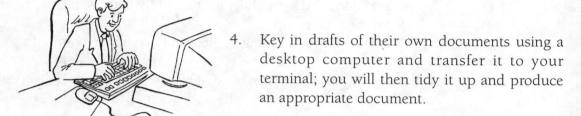

4. Key in drafts of their own documents using a desktop computer and transfer it to your terminal; you will then tidy it up and produce an appropriate document.

"No honestly, I wasn't talking to myself at all. I was dictating!"

Many employers are looking forward to a time when they can speak into a word processor or computer and words are created. This technology is restricted to certain words and phrases at the moment but it is not impossible to think that fairly soon full text creation will be possible through voice input.

Methods used for transcribing documentation will vary from company to company, but fortunately the days of manual typewriters are long gone; even electric typewriters are not very common now. Although there is a very wide range of electronic typewriters currently available, the common trend is for the secretary to have a word processing system. It is important that you keep yourself up-to-date with the latest equipment and programs so that you can easily transfer your skills when your company introduces new technology or if you move to a different company.

Check it out! How do employers in your company prefer to pass on work to their secretaries? Do the methods vary throughout your region/country? Discuss the advantages and disadvantages of each method and make notes for your file.

Business Correspondence

Today's secretary may be required to produce a wide range of business documents, from letters and memos to complicated forms and publicity leaflets. It is not intended in this workbook to look at the principles of effective communication or to discuss the many documents which a secretary may have to transcribe. It is expected that detailed attention will be given to composition of all such correspondence in Transcription and Business Communication lessons.

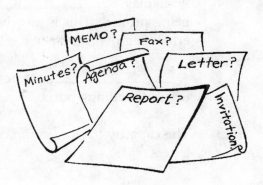

However, you may be required to produce written communications in your Secretarial Duties examinations so do remember the 'one rule for all' principle. Whatever layout you use, and whether producing handwritten or typewritten documents, consistency should be your key.

Guidelines for composition and specimen formats of the most commonly-used business documents appear in **Communication for Business - A Practical Approach** and also in **Model Business Letters.**

Typewriters

When electric typewriters took over from manuals they were popular because of their even touch which required less physical effort, also repeater keys speed up work and the different type faces and pitch enhanced the appearance of work.

Special circuit boards and silicon chips were then used to control the keyboard of electronic typewriters. This typewriter is quieter to operate and can perform many special functions. Can you name some of these functions and write them in the boxes below?

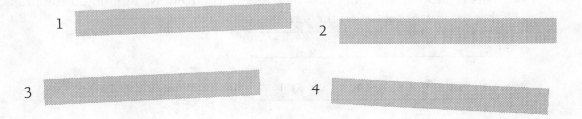

1   2

3   4

The latest electronic typewriters also have additional features. Fill in the blanks below.

1   A display _____ showing a certain number of characters before being printed. This is an advantage because the secretary can _____ errors before printing.

2   A _____ store ranging from a few lines to several pages. This is useful for editing purposes.

3   The capacity to store commonly used _____ for forms and standard letters.

Screen-Based Systems

Many screen-based systems are now available, and they incorporate several features. Choose the appropriate word from the box to label the diagram of a modern system.

> CPU (Central Processing Unit)
> Mouse
> Cursor
> Printer
> Disks
> Keyboard
> Screen or VDU (Visual Display Unit)

1   This has special function keys to centralise text, embolden, change the print size or type, etc.

2   This displays several lines of text which is easily edited before printing.

3   This usually flashes to indicate the point on screen where information will appear.

4   This is another input device which allows you to move around on the desktop so that the cursor moves on the screen.

5   This is the brains of the whole system. There may be one or two drives.

6   The documents processed on screen can be stored in these.

7   The paper copy of your work is very important so choose appropriate quality for
this important piece of equipment.

Printers

There are four main types of printer. Which type is being
described here?

1   This printhead is circular with characters on the end
of each 'spike'. It produces work similar to typing.
Many printheads are available for different typestyles
and pitch (or size). Printing may be bi-directional.

2   With this system characters are formed by a series of
dots. This is quite fast but the work is not of a very
high quality.

3   This produces very high quality printing. Ink is forced
out at very high speed, forming characters on the
paper. Work can even be produced in several colours.

4   The highest quality work is produced by this type of
printer, which uses a high energy light beam to print.

Check it out!   Visit some local shops and pick up some leaflets on printers. Cut out
examples of the different printheads and make a poster for your
classroom wall.

Choosing a Printer

The choice of printer will generally depend on the quality of work required. The table below compares daisy wheel and dot matrix printers. Discuss the same categories in relation to the ink jet and laser printers and complete the table.

	Daisy wheel	Dot matrix	Ink Jet	Laser
Speed	Slow (20–55 cps)	Quite slow		
Quality	High	Usually poor but can vary		
Fonts	Change disks to vary	Limited flexibility		
Noise factor	Very noisy	Noisy		
Cost	Cheaper	More expensive		
Other considerations	Disks break if used carelessly	Uses colour		

Floppy Disks

The most popular medium for storing information are floppy disks which come in two sizes, flexible disks 5 1/2" and solid disks 3 1/4". All floppy disks should be handled with special care.

Choose appropriate words to complete the sentences below.

1   Always _____ disks to show the contents.

2   Keep disks in their protective _____ when not in use.

3   Insert disks into drives in the correct _____.

4   Keep disks away from high _____.

5   Keep disks flat and do not _____ or fold disks.

6   Keep disks away from _____ equipment which may corrupt the memory.

7   Do not use _____ on disks.

8   Do not _____ the portion of disk which is exposed.

Ergonomics and VDU Regulations

Ergonomics is the study of the compatibility of people, equipment and environments. As comfort and productivity are closely linked, this issue is important if efficiency is to be ensured. Can you name some factors which could lead to occupational stress and therefore reduce efficiency? Write these factors in the box below.

_____   _____

_____   _____

_____   _____

Many VDU operators suffer headaches, backache, eyestrain, mental stress and other problems. Such fatigue often affects efficiency. Steps which should be taken to avoid the risks involved in using VDUs are set out in the *Health and Safety (Display Screen Equipment) Regulations 1992*. These regulations affect employed and self-employed workers who use VDUs regularly for a lot of their routine work.

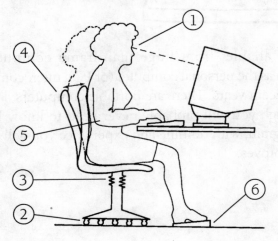

An ergonomically designed workstation can reduce these risks. Discuss the important features of such a workstation shown in the diagram. Make notes on the next page.

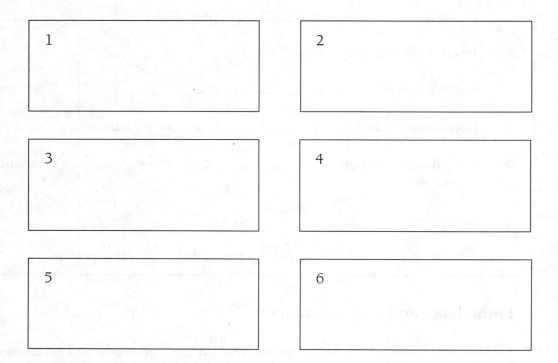

Computer Technology

Computer technology is being developed at an alarming rate and the changes are almost impossible to keep up with. However, most office workers should understand the basics of computer technology.

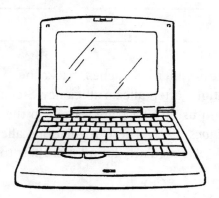

Many types of computer are available, from huge mainframe computers to microcomputers. Otherwise known as the personal computer (or PC), microcomputers have developed tremendously in recent years. There are portable computers, laptops, notebooks, even palmtops. Although you will probably never need to know how to program a computer or write a program, with training and experience you will extend your knowledge as technology improves.

Integrated Packages

Most secretaries use an integrated package rather than a dedicated word processor. Integrated software is often sold as a package and they are less expensive than buying each component separately. Content may vary and the choice will depend on the extent of your particular job. Choose the correct application program from this box to label the following descriptions.

Electronic mail	Graphics	Desktop Publishing
Database	Spreadsheets	Organiser

1 _____

Rows and columns are shown on this electronic worksheet. Common uses of this type of application are payroll, expense accounts, stock control, forecasting.

2 _____

This application converts numerical data into charts or graphs, making comparisons and analysis easier. Presentations can be enhanced with eye-catching designs in a variety of colours.

3 _____

This application is used to record information such as names, addresses, personal details, perhaps salaries. Each individual aspect of information is called a field and various fields make up one record. Data can be sorted according to the various fields.

4 _____

Using this software, computer users can send messages to other users on the same network. Messages are stored in a mailbox until the user is ready to read his/her mail. A hard copy may be printed before the message is deleted from the screen. Replies can be sent immediately.

5 _____

This application is used when designing pages for inhouse printing. Use columns, lines and artwork, different styles and sizes of print, all on one page.

6 _____

Secretaries will find this useful in managing her own and her employer's diaries. Meetings can be plotted, deadlines noted and future events planned. Some packages also include calculators and telephone diallers.

Input Methods

The keyboard and the mouse have already been discussed, but there are other methods which could be used to input information into a computer. Can you identify the methods from the descriptions given?

1 _____

or OCR

A special device scans over typed or printed details, and using light-based technology the information is automatically read by the computer. This saves keying in all the information.

2 _____

An optical wand called a light pen scans these bars and they are automatically converted into a form which the computer understands. You probably see this happening every day when you go shopping.

6 901009 119301

3 _____

Making a selection from the screen is easy; simply touch the appropriate section or symbol shown on the VDU.

4 _____

With the relevant software package these devices are used to trace a sketch onto the screen. They are also commonly used to read bar codes.

5 _____ or MICR

Another scanning device, this time commonly used by banks for sorting cheques. Characters or symbols on special documents are automatically read by the computer.

6 _____

Systems already exist where equipment can recognise words or instructions but this method is presently very limited. Research is continuing into this exciting area and systems will continue to be improved constantly.

The Data Protection Act

Technological developments mean that a great deal of information about individuals can be stored on computer. Such information can be accessed easily and quickly. However, the rights of individuals are protected by the *Data Protection Act* which came into force in 1984. This law protects the misuse of computer-based information about individuals and lays down rules regarding the processing of such information.

Electronic Mail

The extent to which companies use the latest technology varies according to size and requirements. One thing is certain: today's businesses operate in a highly competitive market where high-speed communication and information transfer is essential. To meet this growing need, electronic mail has evolved as a result of major advances in two main areas:

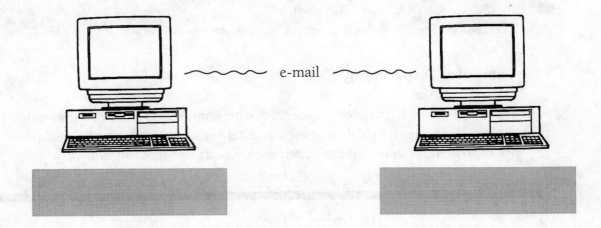

Electronic mail has made instant communications possible not only company-wide but nationwide and worldwide.

We do not necessarily need to understand the way electronic mail uses telephone and computer connections, cables, microwaves, light beams and satellites to make such communication possible. However, as it is unlikely that you will work in an office without e-mail facilities, an appreciation of the concept of e-mail and its various applications is essential.

Telegrams, telemessages, telex and fax are among the commonly used e-mail services. However, on a larger scale electronic mail has come to mean computer-based networks. They may operate within an individual department, a company, a country or internationally across the globe. Each terminal has a built-in mailbox and messages can be sent or received instantly. Messages may also be transmitted to several users at the same time.

This diagram shows how many pieces of electronic equipment are linked together on a local area network (LAN) which operates within a limited area such as an office building. Each device operates independently but may also communicate with others on the system. Common information sources are also shared.

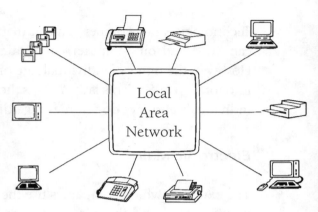

Check it out!   Does your company operate an e-mail system? Discuss the features of the system. Make a list of the advantages and disadvantages of e-mail. Keep notes in your file.

Computer Terminology

There is a lot of terminology associated with computers. A lot of these terms have already been mentioned but some extra terminology is shown here. Choose the appropriate term in the box to match each description that follows.

Bug	Hardware	Modem
LAN (Local Area Network)	Online	Software
Applications Study	GIGO (Garbage In Garbage Out)	Offline
Systems Analyst	Program	WAN (Wide Area Network)

1 _____

Equipment which makes up a computer system.

2 _____

A computer program or applications package.

3 _____

A set of instructions written in a special language which the computer follows.

4 _____

A study which is carried out to determine the programs, equipment and costs involved in dealing with a specific procedure with computer technology.

5 _____

A person who analyses business systems and recommends the type of computer and the programs required to perform the necessary tasks.

6 _____

An error or malfunction which prevents a program from working properly.

7 _____

This can relate to a printer or other piece of equipment which is not directly connected to the main computer system.

8 _____

This describes any process which sends information directly to a computer for immediate processing.

9 _____

This device allows information to be transmitted digitally through the telephone network. The term is short for modulator-demodulator.

10 _____

Using this system electronic equipment within a limited area (such as an office building) is linked together by using cabling.

11 _____

This network extends beyond a single building. It may cover a region or a country. Some networks even operate internationally.

12 _____

This term is used to remind you that if incorrect and faulty data is put into a computer, the output will also be incorrect and faulty.

Quick Quiz

Processing Information

A   Circle your answers.

1   A cursor is
   a   a pen-shaped input device.
   b   an on-screen indicator which shows the position at which information will be input.
   c   someone who is not very happy.

2   Edit means
   a   to feed information into a computer.
   b   to store information.
   c   to check and revise text.

3   What name is given to a document produced in paper form as opposed to onscreen form?
   a   A business letter
   b   A facsimile
   c   Hard copy

4   This is a telecommunications network which covers a large region or country.
   a   LAN
   b   WAN
   c   PABX

5   This person examines business systems and recommends the computer, programs or other equipment needed.
   a   Systems analyst
   b   Software Manager
   c   Programmer

6   This printer comprises a circular printhead with the typeface on the end of each spike.
   a   Ink Jet
   b   Dot matrix
   c   Daisy wheel

7   This is known as the microprocessor and is the 'brain' of the computer.
a   VDU
b   CPU
c   ROM

8   This term refers to an error in a program which prevents it from working properly.
a   An analyst
b   A bug
c   Offline

9   This application package would be used to design pages for an inhouse newsletter.
a   Desktop publishing
b   Graphics
c   Database

10 This package combines programs such as word processing, spreadsheets, graphics and communications.
a   Dedicated word processor
b   Microprocessor
c   Integrated software

B   Name the equipment being described in the following sentences.

1   High quality printing is produced by this printer which forces ink onto paper at very high speeds.

_____

2   As a computer's internal memory is limited, these should be used as external (or auxiliary) storage.

_____

3   This is the term used to describe the monitor or screen on which work produced on a computer is shown.

_____

4   This is an input device which allows the user to select menu options from icons shown on the screen.

_____

5   This device is used to convert the signals of telephone lines into the digital signals needed by computers so that information can be transmitted.

_____

6   This equipment uses light-based technology to read text automatically and thus avoid the need to key in the information.

_____

7   These are specially imprinted codes which are read automatically by a computer using a light pen.

_____

8   Cabling is used with this network system to link together all the microcomputers within a limited area such as an office building.

_____

9   This is an orbiting device in space which picks up signals from the earth at one point and then transmits them to another point.

_____

10 This is a very small machine useful for business people on the move. Using a modem they can interact with office-based terminals, send messages, retrieve files, etc.

_____

Review

1   Explain the term ergonomics. Why should workstations be ergonomically-designed?

2   You have been using a dedicated word processor. Give reasons why an integrated package would be more useful.

Support Services

3.1 OFFICE STORES AND STATIONERY

An expensive item in any office budget is stationery. Often referred to as 'consumable office supplies', it is essential not to run out of such items. It would also be uneconomical to carry excessive stocks as they could deteriorate or become outdated.

Stationery will normally be controlled by the Office Manager or the Purchasing Manager, but in a small company it may be one of the responsibilities of the secretary.

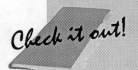

Check it out!   Stationery includes much more than paper. In a brainstorming session, make a long list of items which would come under the heading of 'consumable office supplies'. Keep notes in your file.

Monitoring Supplies

Most companies operate a system called FIFO - this means first in first out. This is particularly important where items have a limited shelf life and could deteriorate quickly.

Supplies are usually issued to staff when they complete a requisition form.

Stationery Requisition

Job No. _____

From _____

To _____

Quantity	Description

Signed _____   Date _____

Stationery Stock Card

Item _____ Maximum Stock _____
_____ Minimum Stock _____

Date	Receipts			Issues			Balance in Stock
	Quantity Received	Invoice No.	Supplier	Quantity Issued	Requisition No.	Department	

When goods have been issued the transaction will be recorded manually on a stock card. This shows the minimum and maximum levels of stock, plus how much stock is currently in hand. You can then reorder before stocks become too low. With modern computer systems, stock can also be controlled using spreadsheets.

Controlling Office Supplies

A good system of controlling office supplies is essential. Discuss this system as you complete the blanks in the list below.

1   Always _____ the stationery store cupboard (or room, depending on the size of the firm).

2   Cupboards must be kept _____, accessible only to a specified person or persons.

3   Some companies lay down _____ times or days for issue of stationery. This prevents the controller from being interrupted constantly during each day.

4   Circulate to all staff a _____ stating times of issuing stationery. Also put this up on the stock cupboard or room door.

5   It is also useful to circulate a list of _____ available.

6 Stock should be _____ at regular intervals, for instance twice a year to make sure the balances on the record cards agree with the quantity on the shelves.

EPOS (Electronic Point of Sale)

Many shops and supermarkets now operate a system of monitoring stocks by scanning goods at the checkout. Discuss how this system works by completing the blanks below.

1   A scanner identifies each product through the _____.

2   Information is transferred to a central _____.

3   Stock is automatically _____ as each item is sold.

4   When the stock level is _____ to a certain level, the goods are automatically reordered.

Benefits of EPOS

1   As stocks are sold they are instantly _____.

2   The risk of _____ and _____ is reduced.

3   The system is quick and _____.

4   Everything is instant; there is no _____.

5   Companies will find it useful to make _____ about sales in certain periods, eg weekly or monthly.

6   Larger companies with many branches can identify variations throughout individual _____.

7   Comparisons in sales can also be identified according to each different _____.

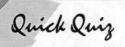

Quick Quiz

Office Stores and Stationery

Answer these questions.

1   Name the form which staff should complete when they need stationery.

_____

2   Stock should not be issued to staff until this form has been ...

_____

3   Why is stock usually issued only at certain times of each day?

_____

4   What is the name give to the record which is kept of each stock item?

_____

5   What happens when the stock of an item falls to the minimum level?

_____

6   Why is a maximum stock level noted?

_____

7   What is the name of the computer program used for monitoring stock records?

_____

8   Using an electronic stock control system, how is he computer informed of stock issued?

_____

9   To avoid deterioration of stock, a system called FIFO is operated. What does this mean?

_____

10   Why is it important to avoid stockpiling?

_____

Review

1 You are responsible for stationery stock control in your company. Explain the system you would use.

2 For what reasons might your company decide to record its stock on databases and monitor stocks using scanners?

As a secretary you should be aware of the various methods of making copies of documents, giving consideration to efficiency and economy. You should also be familiar with the various ways in which documents can be presented or bound.

The use of carbon paper and spirit duplicators is a thing of the past. Even ink duplicating, where a wax stencil was made using a stylus pen or typewriter, is no longer common. However, many companies will have an inhouse printing department with trained operators using offset litho duplicating equipment. Offset lithography is a very professional method of producing large quantities of high-quality documents. What is the copying or duplicating equipment used in your company?

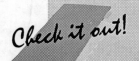 Visit some local equipment stores and collect some leaflets about duplicating equipment. Make a poster for your classroom notice board.

Photocopiers

Most offices today have a photocopier. Many developments have taken place in recent years and the variety of copiers available is extensive. The range covers simple desktop models suitable for producing below 1,000 copies per month, to high volume copiers capable of producing 30,000 to 100,000 copies per month.

Modern photocopiers are easy to use and have many special features. The size and capabilities of photocopier chosen will be determined by the nature of the copying work to be done by individual companies.

Use this mnemonic to name some special features found on modern photocopiers.

C_____

R_____

E_____

S_____

T_____

T_____

Procedures for Copying

Some companies find photocopying costs increasing because of unnecessary copying or uneconomical use of the machine's special features, ie reduction/enlargement/double-sided printing. Misusing the machine can also lead to breakdowns or malfunctions. For these reasons many companies lay down certain procedures for controlling the use of the photocopier. Such procedures are listed below.

1 A simple _____ record is made in a notebook, noting the date, number of copies, name of user, etc.

2 A _____ form is completed by users and authorised by department heads.

3 Plastic _____ or keys issued to each employee are inserted in the photocopier and they count the number of copies made automatically.

4 A _____ code is issued to each user to key into the machine. The number of copies made is automatically registered.

Copyright Laws

The illegal use of copyright materials is of serious concern to authors and publishers. It actually amounts to theft of their property. The *Copyright, Designs and Patents Act 1988* provides severe penalties for the unauthorised copying of printed and published materials and software. Written permission from the copyright holder should be obtained before such materials are reproduced, otherwise legal action could be taken.

Document Presentation

Duplicating or copying documents is an important aspect of office life, but there are other items of equipment and materials which will also help to give a professional appearance to your finished set of papers.

Name the equipment being described here.

1   A _____ cuts papers down to appropriate sizes. Various sizes are available, with protective guards for safety.

2   A _____ helps to put all your papers into a neat stack with all the edges aligned.

3   A _____ arranges the pages according to the page number, making short work of this laborious manual task. Various sizes and capacity areas are available, and this feature is now built into many photocopiers.

4   _____ or _____ equipment will be needed to present sets of documents attractively and professionally. Various types of coloured plastic spines are available or a cover with a title may be used. To secure papers more permanently, use a machine which will punch the papers as well as hold them together in a plastic 'comb' spine.

5   A _____ uses heat bonding to coat documents with a plastic film. This provides protection for documents or posters. They can then easily be kept clean and withstand constant use without deterioration.

Discuss the types of equipment and presentation methods used in your company. Visit your local stationery shops and pick up some leaflets.

Reprographics

A   Answer these questions.

1   Name the equipment and facilities needed to produce many complex diagrams in a variety of different sizes to be incorporated into reports.

_____

2   Your employer has many fact sheets which she wishes to safeguard against deterioration. Suggest how they could be protected.

_____

3   You need to cut some A4 paper down to A5 size. Name the equipment you will use.

_____

4   Before photocopying pages of any book you should check certain legislation in your country. What term is commonly used for this legislation?

_____

5   You need to bind a report with many pages. What method would you suggest?

_____

B   Which function of the photocopier would you use for the following?

1   10 sets of a 30-page document

_____

2   20 pages which must be produced as a 10-page document

_____

3   An A5 size notice to be produced as A4

_____

4   A diagram on A3 which is to be included in an A4 size report

_____

5   A diagram to be shown on overhead projector in a presentation

_____

Review

1   Which equipment would you use in the following situations? Give reasons.

a   You have produced notices for posting around the company and want to ensure they do not deteriorate.

b   You need to bind a multi-page report for your employer to present to all members of the next management meeting.

c   You need to incorporate copies of several complex diagrams into a report but will need to adjust their sizes to fit the space available.

3.3   RECORDS MANAGEMENT

Although filing is often thought to be a boring routine job, finding papers when required is an essential feature of your job. Chaos can result if filing is not carried out efficiently and a missing file or misfiled document could be disastrous. As a secretary you must ensure that your filing system is both efficient and cost-effective.

The following are the features of an efficient filing system.

1   It should be _____ to use.

2   You should be able to _____ documents and files quickly.

3   It should be _____ when the volume of information changes.

4   Documents must be _____ and protected from fire and deterioration.

5   It should be _____ in terms of cost and space.

As a secretary it is important for you to be aware of the methods and principles involved in ensuring that your filing system meets these objectives.

Storage Systems

There are three main types of storage system used for filing. These are vertical, lateral and horizontal. From the illustrations and descriptions below, choose the appropriate name for each system.

1 ____________________

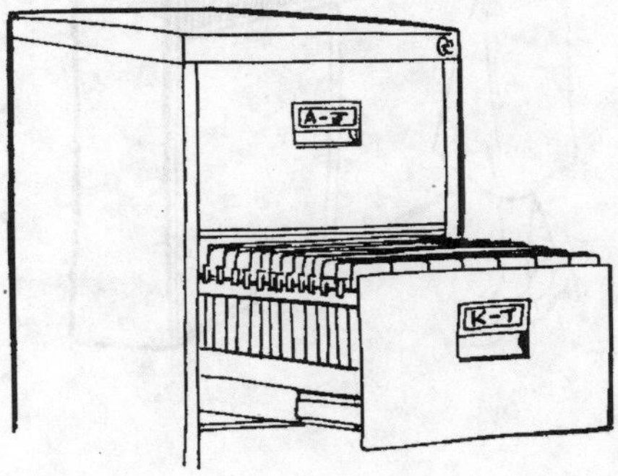

This type of filing system is the most common. Various colours are available for these filing cabinets, which may be 2-, 3- or 4-drawer. Documents are filed in ____________________ files, one hanging behind the other. The title of the file is shown on the spine of each pocket.

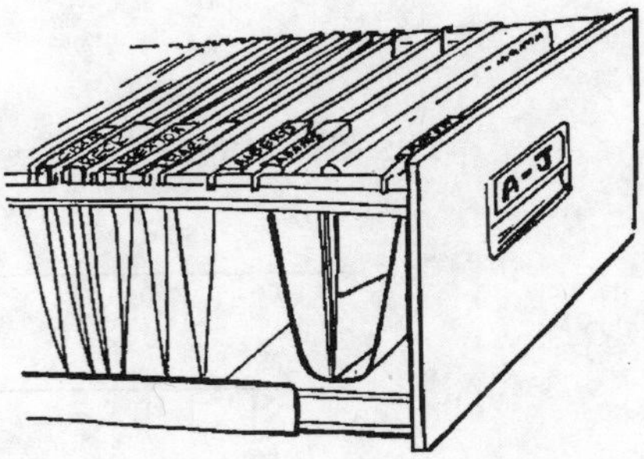

Advantages of this type of storage system are:

- It is ____________________ to use and no special training is needed.
- Filing and retrieval is ____________________ and easy.
- File ____________________ can easily be seen.
- Cabinets can be ____________________ to safeguard files.

Disadvantages are:

- ____________________
- ____________________
- ____________________
- ____________________

2

In this system, files are stored side by side just like books on library shelves. The title of each file is shown on the front edge of the pocket.

Advantages of this type of storage system are:

- It uses _____ very economically.

- Access to files is _____ - no opening drawers.

- Many files can be _____ at one time.

- Many people can have _____ at the same time.

Disadvantages are:

- _____

- _____

- _____

- _____

3

There are various filing systems in this category. The main principle is that documents are laid flat on top of each other. Ring-binders, lever arch files or box files may be used.

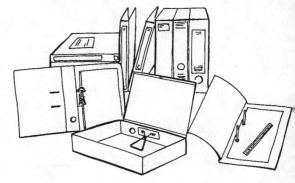

Advantages of this type of storage system are:

- Files and equipment are very _____.

- It is the _____ storage method.

Disadvantages are:

- _____

- _____

- _____

- _____

Filing Classifications

Files can be classified in various ways according to the needs of different departments or organisations. Give the name of each classification as defined below.

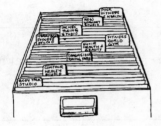

1 _____

This is the simplest and most common method of classification. The surname is the filing point, and when names are identical, refer to the first name or initials.

2 _____

Travel agents may use this classification system. Files are held in alphabetical order according to towns, regions or countries.

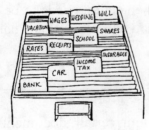

3 _____

Using this method, files are held in alphabetical order according to the subject matter. This method is useful for filing personal papers.

4 _____

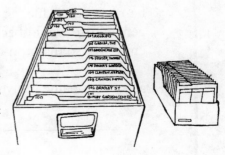

Using this method, each file is given a number and a separate card index is needed to keep record cards in alphabetical order according to names. Insurance companies or banks may use this method.

Check it out! Which type of filing system is used in your company? Discuss the different equipment and classification systems used.

Filing Routines

For a filing system to be efficient, certain procedures need to be followed regarding naming, removal and retention of files. Answer the following questions and discuss these individual procedures.

1   When a document may be relevant to more than one file, a copy may be inserted in each file. What alternative system could be used?

    _____

2   If a file or document is removed, a note should be made of the borrower and the date. What will be inserted in its place?

    _____

3   Some current papers should not be filed immediately because further information is needed. What are such papers called and in what type of storage system would they be held?

    _____

4   Temporary storage may be needed for papers when action needs to be taken in the near future. What is the name of the system you will use so that a daily check can be made of such papers?

    _____

5   There are legal requirements which specify how long certain documents should be retained on file, eg company formation documents, special policies. Files in general use would become very bulky if a procedure was not agreed with your employer so that non-current files are removed to special archive storage.

    a   What name is given to this storage policy?

    _____

b   Give at least three factors which should be considered in deciding on this policy?

_____

_____

_____

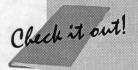

Check it out!

This would be a good opportunity to ensure that your filing system for course notes is up-to-date. Do you have separate binders for each subject? Within each binder are the different topics separated by dividers for easy reference? Are your notes neat and in logical order?
· Be an efficient secretary and tidy your files regularly.

Microfilm Storage

Traditional methods for storing documents are expensive because of the equipment and space required. Microfilming reduces documents to the size of a postage stamp, cutting the amount of storage space required by up to 98 per cent. This system works by filming the original paper documents. Several types of microfilm are available.

1   _____ is a sheet of film which holds 98 micro-images (A4-size images are reduced 24 times).

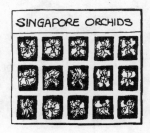

2   _____ cards are frames with pieces of microfilm inset. These are usually used in punched card installations.

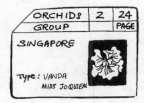

3   _____ of microfilm are more expensive but easier to handle. Cassettes and cartridges of microfilm are also available but again they are more expensive. These systems are time-consuming when locating required sections.

4 _____ or COM are also available. In this system, digital output from a computer is converted to microform without printing on paper first. CIM, or Computer Input on Microfilm, is the reversal of this system, transferring information directly from microforms to the computer.

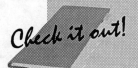

Filming and processing microfilm requires special equipment like the Reader/Printer shown here. Visit some local showrooms and collect some leaflets on microfilming. Keep these in your files or make a wallchart.

Reasons for Microfilming

Discuss why companies would decide to switch to microfilm storage of its records. Think of the disadvantages and complete the table below.

Advantages	Disadvantages
1 Saves space.	
2 Can be carried/ posted easily.	
3 Safety and security is improved.	
4 Can improve efficiency.	

Electronic Filing

With computer technology it is now possible to store massive amounts of information on computer which can be accessed by many people on an area network. The reality of the 'paperless office' also has the inevitable benefits of saving trees and protecting the environment.

Computerised files usually take these two forms:

1   (ROM)

These files are permanently installed in the computer. They can be accessed but not changed.

2   (RAM)

These are files which can be created, accessed and edited.

Check it out! Discuss the advantages and disadvantages of storing information electronically on computer databases. Make notes for your files.

Quick Quiz

Records Management

A   Circle your answers.

1 Your company uses colour coding in its alphabetical filing system as follows:

        A-F Yellow; G-L Red; M-R Black; S-Z Blue

Which colour would be used to denote these names?
Write your answer in the box.

a   St Andrew's College

b   Sir John Smith

c   Lim Lee Fong

2   The main aim of filing is to
    a   store files in a safe place.
    b   find documents quickly.
    c   keep documents clean and tidy.

3   When would a release mark be used?
    a   When a document has been borrowed from the files.
    b   When files are inactive and are transferred to storage.
    c   When a document is finished with and is ready for filing.

4   When a document is relevant to more than one file, a marker may be put in each place. This is called a
    a   cross reference.
    b   pending file.
    c   miscellaneous file.

5   Information can be stored on computer using
    a   microfilm.
    b   electronic filing.
    c   VDU.

B Circle True or False.

1   A pending file is used to make a cross reference with another document.   True / False

2   An Absent Marker is placed in a file when the secretary leaves work to finish off after her lunch break.   True / False

3   When a document has been transferred to microfilm, a hard copy cannot be made.   True / False

4   Suspension files are used with vertical filing cabinets.   True / False

5   A two-ring binder is an example of a lateral filing system. True / False

6   When using the geographical classification system a separate card index in alphabetical order is also needed.   True / False

7   Documents should always be filed in chronological order regardless of the system of classification used.   True / False

8   When non-current files are removed to a separate
    location, this is sometimes known as archive storage.   True / False

9   Papers awaiting replies or further information are kept
    in a cross reference file.   True / False

10 A certificate of authenticity is a document which states
    that the microfilm is a true copy of the original.   True / False

Review

1   It is good policy to have a general code of practice for filing. Write a
    checklist of the points to be remembered so that you can ensure that
    documents are always found when required.

2   a   Why might your company decide to use microfilm?
    b   Explain the meaning of the following terms:
        i   microfiche
        ii   film jacket
        iii aperture card
        iv   CIM

HUMAN RESOURCES

The survival of a company depends on employing the right people and if workers are to be productive and efficient, good staff relations are vital. Most companies lay down specific policies and procedures regarding its employees. These policies are carried out by the Human Resources or Personnel Department.

The activities of this department are many and varied. Use this mnemonic to name them.

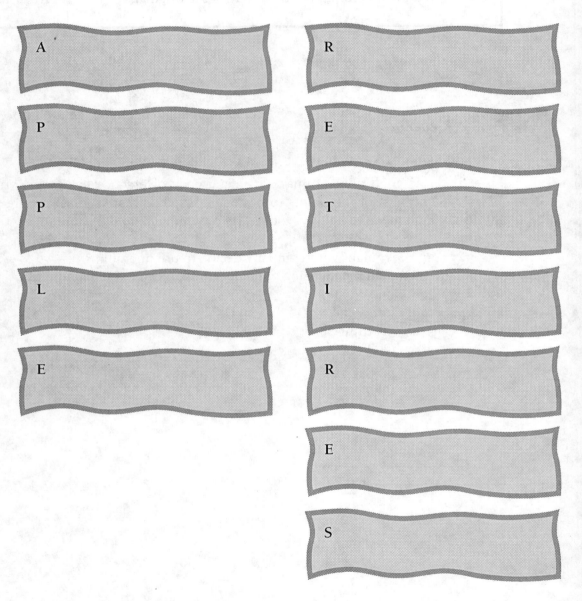

A

P

P

L

E

R

E

T

I

R

E

S

Recruitment and Selection

As a secretary you may be involved in the selection of junior staff or your advice may be sought regarding a suitable replacement if your are promoted. It is important to understand the procedures involved in recruiting staff.

The recruitment and selection process is discussed in the following sentences. Choose words from the shaded portion to complete the sentences. Discuss each stage as you go through them. Could you bring to class examples of any of these documents used in your company?

> personnel specification
>
> testimonials   interviews   job description   second interviews   induction
>
> curriculum vitae   contract of employment
>
> letter of appointment   advertisement   shortlist   references

1 Larger companies have a formal _____ for each employee, listing the duties to be performed by each member of staff.

2 It is useful also to draw up a _____ showing the type of person required for the job, including personal qualities, experience and qualifications.

3 When the appointment has been approved, an _____ is placed in local or national newspapers, perhaps also on the company's notice board.

4 A _____ is usually requested showing the history of an applicant's employment, qualifications and experience as well as personal details.

5 _____ may be taken up by telephoning or writing to the persons named for information regarding an applicant's character or work performance.

6   Some applicants will enclose copies of _____ from former employers which provide useful information.

7   If many applications are received a _____ of potentially suitable applicants must be drawn up.

8   Arrangements must be made to conduct _____ with the chosen applicants. This may involve making phone calls or writing letters.

9   Sometimes _____ will be held so that certain applicants can be interviewed again before a final choice is made.

10   A _____ will be sent to the person chosen, outlining details of the position offered, salary, date for reporting to work, hours of work, holidays, etc.

11   A formal _____ may be issued, setting out the main terms of employment.

12   On the first day of work an _____ course will usually be provided for the new employee to make this preliminary period as smooth as possible.

Check it out!   Refer to your Use of English textbook **Communication for Business – A Practical Approach** for examples of the documents included in the recruitment and selection process.

Fringe Benefits

In addition to salaries, many companies provide 'perks' to employees to make the job more attractive. Such perks may be in the form of goods sold or manufactured by the company. Can you name some other types of fringe benefits? Write them in the space on the next page.

Fringe Benefits:

_____   _____

_____   _____

_____   _____

_____   _____

Preparations for Interviews

In order to ensure successful interviews, certain preparations will be necessary.

1   *Schedule appointments*

     Liaise with other members of staff who may be involved in the interviews, including the person for whom the applicant will work.

2   *Tests*

     If applicants' skills are to be tested, a suitable room should be chosen and materials made available.

3   *Interview room*

     Arrange the room so that applicants can be comfortable. There should be no interruptions.

4   *Waiting areas*

     Applicants may wait in the reception area or in another nominated area. Cloakroom facilities and refreshments may be necessary.

5   *Questions*

     It may be useful to prepare a separate list of questions to ask applicants. (Discuss this and make a separate note of useful questions for your file.)

6   *Documentation*

Make sure you have the following documents so that accurate details can be provided to all applicants.

_____

_____

_____

_____

 What are the current Acts in your country regarding Employment Legislation?

Contracts of Employment

Under UK employment legislation, all full-time employees should receive details of the major terms of their employment contract within 13 weeks of starting work. The contract should be in duplicate, either in the form of a letter or a separate official document. The new employee will sign one copy which will be kept on file and retain the other for reference.

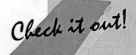 Make a list of items which may be included in a contract of employment. Keep your notes in your file.

Induction Courses

An induction course should be held to familiarise new
employees with the company and to settle them in at
the start of their new employment. Induction courses
may last several days or a few hours depending on the
size and the nature of the company.

"Welcome to Turner Communications."

Can you list the items which will be included in an induction course?

Discuss the steps and preparations involved in arranging a successful
induction course. Make notes for your file.

Staff Development

In an increasingly competitive market, organisations must ensure that their staff are
efficient and productive. A good staff development programme not only ensures this,
it can also build a motivated workforce and high morale.

Just like a proper security policy should not wait until a major break-in occurs, neither
should a staff training and development programme be implemented only when there
is a crisis. Forward thinking organisations will incorporate such a programme into
their overall manpower plan so that potential needs are identified and suitable
programmes compiled.

Training programmes may be organised in-house or staff may be encouraged to attend
programmes run by external training agencies. Such external training providers will
offer both standard programmes as well as design courses, workshops and seminars to
meet individual requirements.

Check it out! Do you know of any specialist training agencies in your locality? What sort of programmes are available for different categories of staff? Make notes for your file.

Staff Appraisal

A record of the progress of all employees should be maintained. This will be especially useful when considering promotion or salary increases and in identifying training needs. Many companies implement a formal annual appraisal scheme for all employees using a special appraisal sheet devised for this purpose.

Suggest some categories in which an employee's performance may be judged in an annual appraisal.

> ✓ _____   ✓ _____
>
> ✓ _____   ✓ _____
>
> ✓ _____   ✓ _____

Discuss the many benefits to be gained from implementing a staff appraisal system as you complete the sentences below.

1 It provides an opportunity for _____ between the employer and the employee.

2 _____ can be provided by the employer about how he/she feels the employee is performing; the employee may also say how they feel they have performed.

3 Any _____ or grievances can be discussed and hopefully resolved.

4 The appraisal may identify _____ which might be necessary.

5 Future prospects regarding _____ can be discussed.

6 A good staff appraisal scheme usually improves _____ and _____.

Does your company have an employee appraisal system? Bring in an appraisal form to put up on your notice board.

What systems are followed in your company regarding disciplinary/grievance/dismissal procedures?

Quick Quiz

Human Resources

A   Circle your answers.

1   The document which details the duties to be performed by each member of staff is called a
a   Testimonial.
b   Job Specification.
c   Job Description.

2   The type of person required for the job is described on the
a   Curriculum Vitae.
b   Reference.
c   Personnel Specification.

3   Applicants usually submit a document showing full details of their employment history, qualifications and employment. This is called a
a   Curriculum Vitae.
b   Letter of Application.
c   Contract of Employment.

4   Fringe benefits are
a   the advantages of working for a hairdresser.
b   supplements provided to employees as incentives.
c   allowances made for working in the personnel department.

5   A shortlist is
a   a document describing the qualities expected in a potential employee.
b   a list of applicants to be interviewed for a job.
c   a term used to describe a poor response to a job advertisement.

1   Recruiting and selecting staff is the sole function of the Personnel Department.

True / False

2   Screening describes the process of narrowing down applicants so that only the most appropriate candidates are interviewed.

True / False

3   An employee in the UK must receive a contract of employment within 13 weeks of starting a job.

True / False

4   A contract of employment must be a formal document rather than in the form of a letter.

True / False

5   A company has the right to dismiss instantly an employee who has broken a company rule.

True / False

6   Induction Training is orientation given to all new employees at the beginning of their employment.

True / False

7   A reference is a letter provided when you leave a company so that you can send a copy to potential employers.

True / False

8   Being provided with subsidised meals in the staff canteen is not usually considered a fringe benefit.

True / False

9   A staff appraisal system is an opportunity for the employer to tell the employee if the company is satisfied with the employee's job performance.

True / False

10   A testimonial is often given to applicants during the interview to test their skills at shorthand/typewriting.

True /False

Review

1   You work for the Personnel Manager of a medium-sized company and he is recommending that the company should transfer employees to a flexible fringe benefit system. Under the scheme, employees would choose fringe benefits up to a value to be agreed by the Board.

    a Why should the company adopt such a scheme?
    b List some fringe benefits which may be available to staff.

2   The Office Manager has been promoted to Director of Office Services. An advertisement is placed in the local newspaper for the post to be filled. Explain the procedures necessary in your department before interviews can be held.

Finance and Statistics

4.1 **WAGES AND SALARIES**

In a small company one of the secretary's responsibilities may be to deal with wages and salaries, but in many companies it may be part of the Personnel Department's function. Larger companies have a special section dealing specifically with payment of wages and salaries. However, you should be familiar with the way in which wages and salaries are calculated.

Do you know the difference between wages and salaries?

Wages _____

Salary _____

There are several ways of calculating wages and salaries. Make notes as you discuss each method.

1　Time rates _____

_____

2　Piece work _____

_____

3　Commission _____

_____

4　Annual salary _____

_____

Additions

There may be certain additions to an employee's basic salary (gross pay). Can you suggest some?

_____   _____

_____   _____

Deductions

1 *Statutory Deductions*

Every country has their own requirements for statutory deductions to be made by law. Make notes on the statutory deductions which apply in your own country.

_____   _____

_____   _____

2 *Voluntary Deductions*

These deductions are agreed by the employee. Again the type of voluntary contributions vary. Discuss the different voluntary deductions which could be made from your salary.

_____   _____

_____   _____

Pay slips

Pay slips must be issued to all employees showing the gross pay, additions and deductions made and the net pay. Payslips show other information such as:

_____   _____

_____   _____

Methods of Payment

Companies may pay their employees using any of these methods.

1 _____

Some weekly paid employees may be given a pay packet containing all the money due.

2 _____

Employees can take these to their bank and pay them directly into their bank account.

3 _____

In many cases, certainly in larger companies, employees are given their pay advice slip only. The company will make arrangements for salaries to be paid directly into employees' bank accounts.

Quick Quiz

Wages and Salaries

Circle True or False.

1 Time rates are provided to employees who regularly arrive at work punctually.   True / False

2 Under a piece rate system employees are only paid for each article they produce.   True / False

3 When payment is on a commission basis, a salesman will be able to increase his salary substantially by selling large quantities of goods.   True / False

4	Statutory deductions are taken from an employee's salary only with his/ her permission.	True / False
5	Your gross pay is the amount you actually receive after all deductions have been made.	True / False

Review

1 a What factors might be taken into account when deciding on a starting salary for a new employee?

   b What methods might be used to pay salaries to employees?

2 a Explain what is meant by statutory and voluntary deductions and give two examples of each.

   b List four items of additional information which would appear on a pay slip.

4.2 BANKING SERVICES

Most people have a personal account at a bank, post office or building society. It is important to be aware of the different accounts and other banking services which are available both for personal and business customers.

1 _____ Account

This account is for regular use. Money can be paid in and withdrawn easily. Interest is not usually earned on this type of account, although there are exceptions. Cheque books are issued to holders of this type of account.

2 _____ Account

This account earns interest so it is beneficial to leave money in it for a longer period of time.

3 There are several special accounts designed for people who want to leave money in the bank for a specified and longer period. A specified notice of withdrawal will be required but interest will be higher.

Cheques

Current account holders will receive a book of pre-printed cheques. A cheque is an order in writing from the account holder (drawer) telling the bank (drawee) to pay a specified sum of money to the person named (payee). A record is kept on the cheque counterfoil which remains in the cheque book.

A cheque is rarely left 'open' because it can be cashed by anyone holding it. This type of cheque will have no lines drawn across it, or a 'crossing'. Some special crossings are illustrated below. Discuss these crossings and make notes on their uses.

1   General Crossed Cheque

& Co

_____

_____

_____

2   Specific Crossed Cheque

Conference Account

_____

_____

_____

3   Account Payee Only Cheque

A/C Payee

_____

_____

_____

4

This type of cheque is made out for a future date and payment will not be made until that date.

5

This is a cheque which the bank has refused to pay, perhaps because there is not enough money in the drawer's account or because it has not been completed correctly.

6

You can give instructions to the bank to do this if, for example, your cheque book has been lost or stolen.

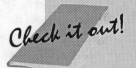

Check it out!

The cheque system and the correct method for completing a cheque varies from country to country. Discuss procedures in your own country.

How would you pay money into an account?

Services Provided to Bank Account Holders

Banks offer many other services to account holders to simplify many common transactions. Match the services in the box with the definitions shown below.

Banker's Draft

Direct Debit   Loan   Credit Transfer (Bank Giro)

Overdraft   Standing Order   Cash Dispensing Machine

1 _____

With this arrangement your bank manager agrees to allow you to spend more money than you have in your account. Interest is usually paid on the amount you are overdrawn.

2 _____

Similar to a cheque, this is sometimes preferred where large amounts are involved because payment is guaranteed by the bank.

3 _____

Written instructions are given to your bank to pay a specified amount from your account on a given day to a named person or organisation. This is useful for regular payments.

4 _____

This is another method of making regular payments but in this case the amount may change each time. This is popular for paying utilities bills where the amount changes each month.

5 _____

This describes a substantial amount of money borrowed over a specified period of time. The bank will charge interest.

6 _____

Use this facility to make cash withdrawals from your account using the special card provided. You will have a personal identity number (PIN).

7 _____

Money is transferred from one account to another by completing a special slip. This system is often used to pay bills to utility companies or salaries to employees.

Bank Statements

Holders of bank accounts will receive regular statements showing all transactions during a specified period (usually a month) together with the balance remaining in the account.

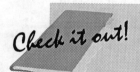 **Check it out!** Discuss a variety of reasons why your bank statement might not agree with the balance shown in your cheque book. Make notes for your file.

Other Banking Services

Banks provide many other services, and it is not always necessary to be an account holder to make use of them. Discuss some other services which are provided by banks.

_____   _____

_____   _____

Credit Cards

Credit cards are not operated by banks but by credit card companies which are linked to banks. The most common credit cards are:

_____

When goods or services are paid for by credit card, the holder will be asked to sign a special slip showing the total charged together with details of the purchase. Details of all purchases are shown on a monthly statement.

Some customers prefer to pay off their monthly credit card bill in full every month so that they are not subject to the high interest charges.

Some companies provide their employees with credit cards as they are very useful when travelling overseas, and avoid the need to carry large sums of money.

Electronic Funds Transfer

Increased use of credit cards has hastened the advent of the cashless society. Customers can now be linked to their banks by using a normal television set, a home computer with a modem and a telephone jack socket. Customers will be able to call up full details of their account, including bank statements and details of standing orders and direct debits. Funds can be transferred at the press of a key. The many benefits of EFT will mean that this system will undoubtedly become one of the most important services provided by the banks.

Discuss the advantages offered by the EFT system.

_____

_____

_____

_____

_____

Electronic Funds Transfer at Point of Sale (EFTPOS)

The need to write a cheque has been eliminated with the introduction of the EFTPOS system. In the UK current account holders may receive a 'Switch' card which is handed to the cashier when payment is requested. The card holder's signature is obtained to verify the payment and funds will be transferred automatically.

Check it out! Is there an EFTPOS system in your country? Is there a difference between your system and the Switch card system in the UK?

Quick Quiz

Banking Services

A   Circle True or False.

1   A current account would be opened if you want to gain interest on money not immediately required.   True / False

2   A cheque which is crossed 'A/C Payee Only' can be cashed across the counter at a bank.   True / False

3   The person who signs a cheque is known as the drawee.   True / False

4   A cheque card is an undertaking by a bank to honour the cheque presented with it (up to a specified limit).   True / False

5   When a cheque is crossed an error has been made and the cheque has been cancelled.   True / False

B   Circle your answers.

1   A book of pre-printed cheques is issued to holders of a
   a   credit card.
   b   current account.
   c   deposit account.

2   An unpresented cheque, dated eight months previously, is known as
    a   open.
    b   endorsed.
    c   stale.

3   A written instruction to the bank to pay a specific amount from your
    account on a specific day to a specific person is known as a
    a   standing order.
    b   direct debit.
    c   credit transfer.

4   When a company has many employees a popular system for paying
    salaries is
    a   cheques.
    b   cash.
    c   bank giro credit.

5   Symbols on cheques are automatically read by computers using which
    input system?
    a   OCR
    b   COM
    c   MICR

Review

1   Briefly explain the difference between the following terms.

    a   Loan and overdraft
    b   Standing order and direct debit
    c   Cheque and banker's draft

2   Name and briefly explain three different methods of paying for goods
    which do not involve cash or cheques.

A secretary in a smaller company may be responsible for maintaining a petty cash system. Even if you are not directly involved in operating the system, you should be familiar with the procedures involved.

Petty cash is used for small payments on office sundries. Rearrange the letters in the words below to reveal items which would be included in payments from petty cash.

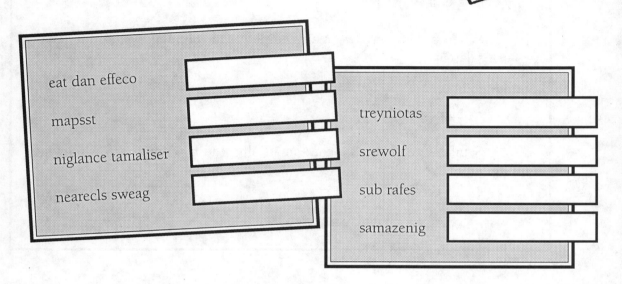

eat dan effeco

mapsst

niglance tamaliser

nearecls sweag

treyniotas

srewolf

sub rafes

samazenig

Petty Cash Flow

Petty cash is operated on a system known as the imprest system. The procedure is described in the sentences below. Choose words from this box to complete the sentences.

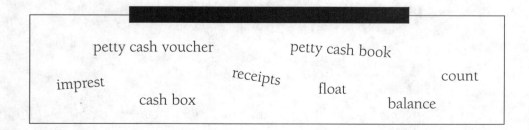

petty cash voucher   petty cash book

imprest   receipts   count
      cash box   float
                                        balance

1   The cashier will give you a _____ known as the imprest.

2   The money should be kept locked away in a _____.

3   _____ must be obtained for all payments made.

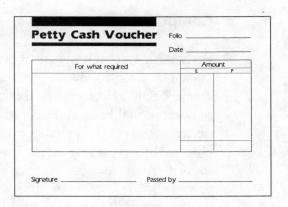

Petty Cash Voucher

| | Folio _____ |
| | Date _____ |

For what required	Amount
	£	P

Signature _____   Passed by _____

4 Each transaction should be recorded on a _____ which must be authorised before payment is made.

5 Details are transferred to the _____.

6 At the end of the month _____ the money left in the cash box.

7 The amount left in the cash box and the amount shown on the petty cash book should _____.

8 Ask the cashier for funds to restore the _____ to its original amount.

Petty Cash Book

A petty cash book records all expenditure made through petty cash. Label this typical page from a petty cash book.

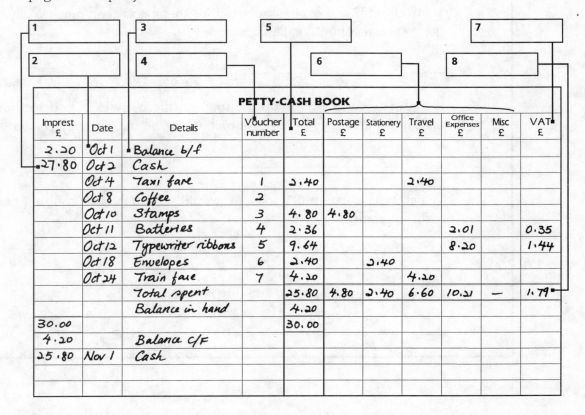

| 1 | | 3 | | 5 | | | | 7 | |
| 2 | | 4 | | | 6 | | | 8 | |

PETTY-CASH BOOK

Imprest £	Date	Details	Voucher number	Total £	Postage £	Stationery £	Travel £	Office Expenses £	Misc £	VAT £
2.20	Oct 1	Balance b/f								
27.80	Oct 2	Cash								
	Oct 4	Taxi fare	1	2.40			2.40			
	Oct 8	Coffee	2							
	Oct 10	Stamps	3	4.80	4.80					
	Oct 11	Batteries	4	2.36				2.01		0.35
	Oct 12	Typewriter ribbons	5	9.64				8.20		1.44
	Oct 18	Envelopes	6	2.40		2.40				
	Oct 24	Train fare	7	4.20			4.20			
		Total spent		25.80	4.80	2.40	6.60	10.21	—	1.79
		Balance in hand		4.20						
30.00				30.00						
4.20		Balance c/F								
25.80	Nov 1	Cash								

Computerisation

Petty cash transactions can be recorded on computer using modern spreadsheet packages. Cash received is recorded in one column while other columns are used to record details of amounts paid out in various categories just like in the analysis columns of a traditional Petty Cash Book. Running totals are calculated automatically. Using a network system the petty cashier can send an e-mail message to the mailbox of the chief cashier reporting on the monies spent and asking for the imprest to be restored to its original amount.

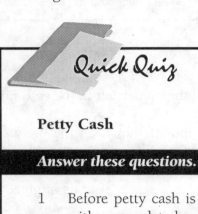

Quick Quiz

Petty Cash

Answer these questions.

1   Before petty cash is issued, what must an employee produce together with a completed petty cash voucher?

_____

2   Each item on a Petty Cash Sheet must be entered twice, first in the 'total' column and again under one of the special columns. What are these special columns called?

_____

3   If the petty cashier adds up the total on the petty cash vouchers and adds it to the money in her cash box, what will the final amount equal?

_____

4   Which type of computer software would be suitable for running petty cash programs?

_____

5   Can petty cash be used for any purchase for the office?

_____

Review

1   a   When a member of staff submits a petty cash voucher, what checks will you make before issuing the cash?

    b   Why might the money left in your cash box not agree with the balance shown in the petty cash book?

2   a   Explain how the imprest system works.

    b   Give six headings which may be found on a petty cash sheet.

GRAPHICAL PRESENTATION

"One picture is worth a thousand words" (Confucius)

In business reports are required all the time, and management information is very often presented in the form of charts and graphs. The most obvious benefit is that visual presentation has a much more immediate impact than words and figures.

This area of computer technology has been developed greatly. Computer graphics can be used to present information in a variety of different ways. Results may be displayed on the screen or printed out to provide a paper copy. Colour may be used to enhance presentation. Such high-quality graphics improve communications in many companies by presenting information in a visual format which is easy to understand. Managers welcome the prospect of making high quality presentations internally, in company reports and literature as well as in presentations to clients.

Regardless of whether you have access to graphics software, you may be asked to suggest the best way of presenting certain types of information, so it is important to be familiar with the various methods.

The main types of visual display are described below.

1

This graph is useful for showing trends over a period of time, eg sales of a certain product.

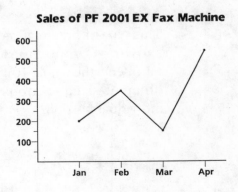

Sales of PF 2001 EX Fax Machine

Sales of PF 2001 EX

KEY
— Northern
--- Southern

Jan	Feb	Mar	Apr	

2

Similar but more complicated, this may be used to show sales of the same product over several sales areas.

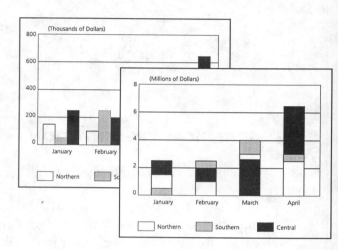

(Thousands of Dollars)

Northern | Southern

(Millions of Dollars)

Northern | Southern | Central

3

This type of display is useful for making comparisons.

		Jan	Feb	Mar	Apr	May	Jun	Jul	Aug	Sep	Oct	Nov	Dec	Jan	Feb	Mar
Housing Development A	Plan															
	Actual time															
Housing Development B	Plan															
	Actual time															

4

This chart would be used to compare planned and actual performance. The top line shows planned progress and the lower line shows actual performance.

5

This type of presentation is useful for showing proportions. A circle represents the whole 100 per cent and different-sized sections show each individual portion.

Co-ordinating and arranging travel, meetings and other functions

Preparation and transcription of documents

General office routines

Telephone skills

Filing and finding

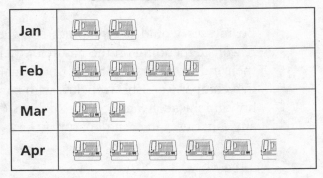

SALES OF PF 2001 EX

Jan	
Feb	
Mar	
Apr	

= **100 Fax machines sold**

6

Symbols or pictures are used to represent a certain number of items. This type of display cannot show specific details, only very general trends.

Examination Approach

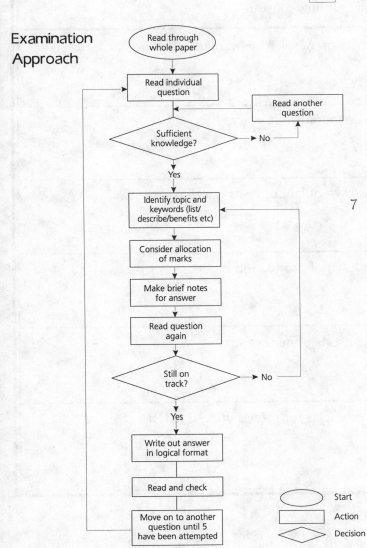

7

This shows the different steps involved in a certain routine. Activities are joined by arrows showing the sequence of steps involved in the procedure.

Graphics Software in Action

Businesses would use graphics software for different reasons depending on the nature of their business and their individual needs. Some of the main departments in a company are shown below with some examples of how graphics software could help them. Can you suggest any other uses in each department?

Department	Use of graphics software
Sales	Comparison of sales by branch or region
Accounts	Breakdown of profit by product
Personnel	Breakdown of labour costs per department
Production	Breakdown of production costs
Marketing	Comparisons of market share
Management	Transparencies for presentation on OHP

 *Check it out!* Information is often portrayed visually in newspapers and magazines. Find some examples in recent issues and make a poster for your notice board.

Desktop Publishing

Visual and graphics are used extensively in desktop publishing, one of the fastest growing technological developments in recent years. Traditionally a specialist printing company had to be employed to typeset and produce special company literature, for example catalogues, brochures, house magazines. Desktop publishing operators design electronic pages using a combination of text, photographs, illustrations, graphs, charts, ruled tables, etc. Eye-catching, attractive and highly professional documents can be produced.

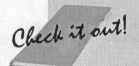

Does your company have a desktop publishing system? Have you used DTP software? Can you bring in some examples to discuss with your classmates?

Statistical records

A   Circle True or False.

1   The sections of a pie chart are normally shown as fractions.　　　　　True /False

2   A bar chart would be used to compare planned and actual performance.　　　　　True / False

3   Bar charts are used in hospitals to show at a glance the temperatures of patients.　　　　　True / False

4   Government statistics are often presented in the form of a pictogram so that the information is made more interesting and understandable.　　　　　True / False

5   A sequence of activities is usually presented as a Gantt chart.　　　　　True / False

1   To compare totals at different points in time.

_____

2   To record actual performance against plan.

_____

3   To show trends over a timescale.

_____

4   To show a sequence of activities.

_____

5   To show relationships of different parts to a whole.

_____

Review

1   List the advantages of displaying information visually.

2   You need to create a line graph comparing sales of your company's products in the Far East and Australian markets. Why would you use a spreadsheet for this?

3   Your company is considering introducing desktop publishing to produce its newsletter.

a   What is desktop publishing?
b   What are the benefits of such a publication?

Part 2:

Secretarial
Procedures

Organisation Skills

5.1 MEETINGS

Most executives spend a great deal of time in meetings, whether they are informal discussions between two or three people or large gatherings taking weeks to plan and requiring endless reports.

In the plan below, complete the blanks with the reasons why meetings are held.

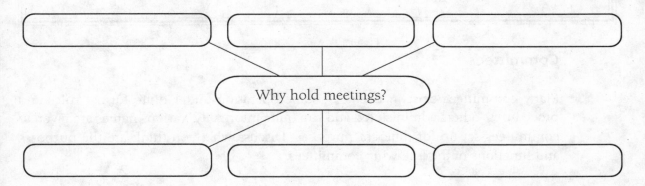

Formal Meetings

Many formal meetings are necessary in business, and they will be conducted in a formal manner with rigid procedures. The names of these meetings are shown in the box. Match the correct name to the descriptions given.

Ordinary General Meeting   Annual General Meeting   Board Meeting

Statutory Meeting   Extraordinary General Meeting

1 _____
This must be held by a company within one to three months of commencing business.

2 _____
This is held every year to report on the company's performance during the period and its current financial position.

3 _____

This meeting will be called if there is special business which needs to be discussed and an Annual General Meeting is not due.

4 _____

This will be called if an interval of one year is thought to be too long before public meetings, or where more active participation is considered essential.

5 _____

Members of this executive committee possess authority to make decisions and take actions. They meet regularly to discuss the day-to-day running of the company. Work is often delegated to less formal committees which report back to this main group.

Committees

Many committees exist in business, some operating under quite formal rules and procedures, others administered and run quite informally. Various names are given to committees set up for different purposes. Discuss what you think are the purposes and functions of the following committees.

1   Standing Committee _____

_____

_____

2   Sub Committee _____

_____

_____

3   Special Purposes Committee _____

_____

_____

4   Membership Committee _____

_____

_____

Check it out!   Are you a member of any social club committees? What types of committee are set up in your company? Discuss their procedures and their responsibilities.

The Chairman

The person who directs a meeting, although sometimes called a Chairperson, is more often referred to as the Chairman, whether male or female. It is his/her duty to direct and control the meeting while remaining as impartial as possible. Can you suggest some special qualities this role demands?

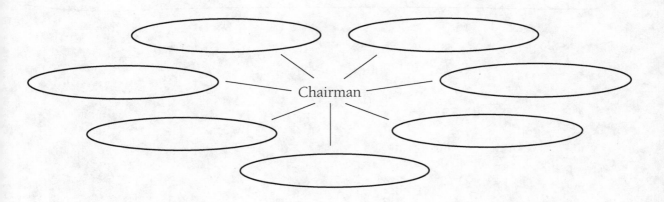

Any Chairman must have an excellent understanding of the function of the committee as well as its powers and authorities. The Chairman's other responsibilities are listed below. Can you fill in the gaps to complete the sentences?

1   Sufficient _____ should be given to all members entitled to attend the meeting.

2   A _____ must be attained, ie the minimum number of members required to make a meeting valid.

3   Business should be conducted in the order of the _____.

4   All members must be allowed _____ opportunity to speak.

5   Discussion should not continue past specific _____ restraints.

6   Members must keep discussion _____ to the point of business.

7   A _____ must be taken if necessary and the result announced by the chairman.

8   A summary of the _____ points should be given at the end of each discussion.

9   The meeting will be _____ after agreeing on a date for the next meeting.

10   _____ of the meeting summarising the discussions must be circulated to all members as soon as possible.

Meetings Documentation

One of the responsibilities of a secretary will be to help the Chairman in preparation of the documentation involved in meetings.

> Specimens of all these documents can be found in your Business English textbook, **Communication for Business - A Practical Approach**. It will be useful to refer to each document as they are discussed in this section.

The main documents are as follows.

1   *Notice and Agenda*

The length of notice which must be given to members required to attend a meeting is usually stipulated in the organisation's rules or constitution. _____ days' notice is required for an Annual General Meeting, but an informal meeting may be held at perhaps a week's notice or even less. The usual wording for the notice is:

_____

_____

The agenda is simply a list of topics to be discussed at a meeting and members will be asked to nominate special items for inclusion on the agenda. However, most meetings will begin and end with certain routine items, known as ordinary business. Can you name these items?

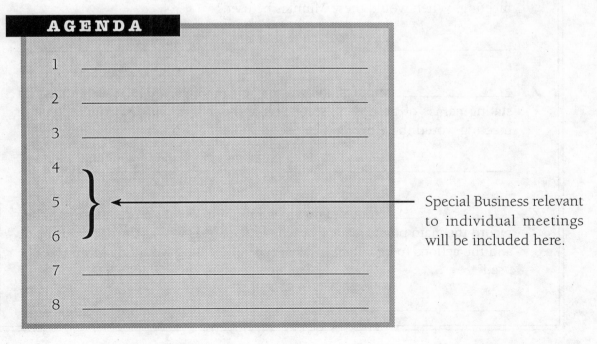

AGENDA

1 _____

2 _____

3 _____

4

5 } ⟵———————— Special Business relevant

6   to individual meetings will be included here.

7 _____

8 _____

2   *Chairman's Agenda*

In order to control the meeting effectively the Chairman needs a special agenda. Refer to an example of this document in your textbook **Communication for Business – A Practical Approach** and state how the Chairman's agenda differs from the members' agenda.

_____

_____

3   *Minutes*

It is important to keep a record of the business conducted at meetings and a secretary may attend meetings to take notes. Minutes will be circulated to all members who attended the meeting as well as those who were absent.

As the minutes report on discussions which have been held and decisions which have been made, what style of writing should be used for the minutes?

When writing minutes use

_____ and _____

There are three different types of minutes.

✓   _____ Minutes are a word-for-word account of everything said at a meeting. When would these Minutes be used?

_____

✓   _____ Minutes, known as short minutes, are formal minutes just stating names of proposers, seconders and decisions made. In what type of meeting would these minutes be used?

_____

✓   _____ Minutes, known as full minutes, are more informal. They record the main points made by each participant as well as the decisions made and the actions to be taken. In what type of meeting would these minutes be used?

_____

Meeting Terminology

There are many formal terms and phrases connected with meetings, and you should be familiar with them. Some of these terms are represented in the following mnemonic. The number of letters in each word has been indicated by the number of squares. Discuss and define each term as you complete the blanks.

A ☐☐☐☐☐☐☐☐☐
☐☐☐☐☐ N
☐☐☐☐ Y

O ☐☐ ☐☐ ☐☐☐☐☐
☐☐ ☐☐ T
☐☐ H ☐☐
E ☐ ☐☐☐☐☐☐
R ☐☐☐☐☐☐☐☐☐

B ☐☐☐☐☐
U ☐☐☐☐ ☐☐☐☐☐
☐☐☐☐☐ ☐☐☐☐☐ S
I ☐ ☐☐☐☐☐☐
N ☐☐ ☐☐☐
☐☐☐☐☐☐ E
S ☐☐☐☐☐☐☐ ☐☐☐☐☐☐
S ☐☐☐ ☐☐☐

Check it out! Look at other reference books and make notes of any other commonly-used terminology associated with meetings. Keep notes in your file.

The Secretary's Responsibilities

The meeting secretary must ensure that meetings are organised and administered efficiently.

The secretary's responsibilities can be divided into the following categories.

1   Preparatory arrangements to be made well in advance
2   Practical arrangements on the day before the meeting
3   Meeting day essentials
4   After the meeting

Checklists are shown here outlining your responsibilities under the first two categories.

Well in Advance

1   Book a room and if necessary confirm in writing.

2   Note details of meeting in diaries (own and employer's).

3   Open a file in which to keep all papers concerning the meeting.

4   Draft notice and agenda for Chairman's approval.

5   Circulate to all members minutes of last meeting (if not already sent) plus any special reports.

6   Make a provisional order for refreshments if required.

Day before the Meeting

1   Confirm refreshments.

2   Prepare items which will be needed by members:
    - pens
    - spare paper
    - spare documents
    - minute/attendance books

3   Sort correspondence and reports for the meeting.

4   Prepare the Chairman's Agenda.

5   Arrange for equipment which may be required, such as:
    - visual aids
    - overhead projector
    - flip chart
    - slide projector

*Check it out!* Discuss the secretary's responsibilities in each of the remaining two categories ('Meeting day essential' and 'After the meeting'). Write out separate checklists for your files. Some words which should be included in your checklists are shown in this box. Some words may be used more than once. You may find it useful to begin each point with a verb but always write in full sentences.

clear/tidy   receptionist   action lists   refreshments

place names   direction signs   distribute

draft

reports   Meeting in Progress   spare copies   approval

equipment   Attendance Book

diaries   Minute Book

seating   ventilation/air-conditioning

additional items   minutes

*Quick Quiz*

Meetings

A   Circle your answers.

1   The Chairman's role is to
    a   keep all members in order.
    b   give his opinions.
    c   direct and control the meeting.

2   What should be the first item on an agenda?
    a   Minutes of the last meeting
    b   Apologies for absence
    c   Matters arising

3   What should be the final item on an agenda?
    a   Date of next meeting
    b   Any other business
    c   Minutes of the last meeting

4   Minutes of Resolution are
     a   fuller minutes, recording all discussions as well as decisions made.
     b   shorter minutes, recording only main points.
     c   word-for-word account of proceedings.

5   A proxy is
     a   a non-member who is asked to attend a meeting to give his/her specialist knowledge.
     b   a person allowed to vote on behalf of another member.
     c   a member of a committee who abstains from voting.

B   Choose appropriate terminology to complete these sentences.

1   Our Company Secretary is to be _____ onto the committee when we discuss legal implications concerning the new project.

2   The meeting cannot be held as there are only four members and this does not constitute a _____.

3   Two members abstained but ten members voted in favour of the motion so it was resolved _____.

4   The meeting will be held _____ as the subjects under discussion are very confidential.

5   To avoid embarrassment, voting will take place by _____.

Review

1   a   As the secretary to the Personnel Manager of Turner Communications, your employer has asked you to compile a notice and agenda for the next monthly department meeting to be held at 1400 next Friday in the Committee Room. Special items for discussion are:

         i   Retirement presentation for Mr Robin Street, Sales Director
         ii   Annual staff appraisal procedures
         iii   Administration staff training programme

     b   As Chairman of the meeting, what are your employer's duties?

5.2   CONFERENCES

Conferences and other major functions bring together people from different departments, companies, and even different countries. Such functions provide a good opportunity to make important contacts in a less pressurised environment away from day-to-day responsibilities.

There could be any number of reasons for holding a major function. List some.

_____ _____

_____ _____

_____

Check it out!   Have you attended a seminar or conference? Bring in the programme and other materials to show your colleagues.

Planning a Conference

As a secretary it is possible that you will be responsible for planning a large function of some kind. Alternatively, you may be part of a team who share the responsibilities. Such planning normally starts several months before the event and will differ according to the nature of the individual function. However, these general guidelines can be adapted to suit most circumstances.

The organisation of large functions falls into six general categories and in this mnemonic, the initial letter of the category has been provided. Can you name the categories?

C_____

A_____

S_____

P_____

E_____

R_____

A systematic approach is vital but to help with current planning it will probably be useful to look at files on previous conferences. A checklist of actions unique to a specific function can then be drawn up so that you can check off items as they are dealt with.

Costing

A budget will have to be agreed by a senior manager, making allowances for all expenses likely to be incurred and any income from bookings for a fee-paying event.

Accommodation

The venue chosen will depend on individual requirements. Larger companies may have in-house conference facilities; otherwise many hotels offer all the facilities and services necessary to ensure the smooth running of your function. Overnight accommodation may also be required for delegates, so this should also be considered when choosing a venue. This process will often involve writing letters of enquiry and visiting potential venues before confirming reservations in writing.

Many factors must be considered in choosing a suitable venue and accommodation. List some of them below.

```
_____        _____

_____        _____

_____        _____
```

Schedule (or Programme) and other Conference Material

An outline programme is probably one of the first things to be drafted. Timings and details may change so it will not be printed until all the details are finalised. In-house printing may be used, but the programme should set out the details as clearly and attractively as possible.

What other conference material may be necessary for a large function?

```
_____        _____

_____        _____

_____        _____
```

Participants

Speakers

Initially you may write a letter giving a speaker full details about the conference which they can then consider before making a decision. Speakers will need to know:

```
_____        _____


_____        _____
```

When a speaker has accepted, you must ask for certain information to be provided. This may include:

_____

_____

Delegates

Details included in the invitations to delegates must be considered carefully so that nothing is omitted. Imagine receiving 200 telephone calls asking where the conference is to be held because you forgot to mention it on the invitation? A tear-off slip or reply form is usually included to standardise replies.

Press

If the conference is being held to promote a new product, representatives of the media may be invited. What documentation might this involve?

_____

_____

Equipment (and other Aids)

The venue should be able to provide all the equipment needed but availability should be checked in advance. Presentation aids could include:

_____   _____

_____   _____

_____   _____

Refreshments (and Meals)

Catering details and the venue will have been discussed and built into the draft programme. A refreshment break will probably be included between the morning and afternoon sessions and buffet style lunches are popular at large functions. Dinner must also be considered and arranged, whether à la carte, buffet or banquet. Remember to take account of special religious or dietary requirements.

Conference Day

In the days leading up to the function you will probably visit the venue to ensure everything is being arranged in accordance with your requirements. When the actual day finally comes around, you will need to be there early to check on all the practical arrangements. During the function you may act as hostess or play a part in receiving guests or delegates. You will certainly be on hand to answer any queries or make any organisational decisions.

Check it out! When you arrive to check the venue on conference day, you will need to bear in mind a few things. Make two checklists to remind you of what to check in the function room (eg is the seating arrangement correct?) and in the registration area (eg is there a name list of the delegates attending the conference?) Keep your notes in your file.

Follow-up

Finally it is over and you will probably breathe a huge sigh of relief, but a great deal of satisfaction can be obtained when you look back on a successful function. However, before you can pat yourself on the back, a certain amount of follow-up must be dealt with.

The mnemonic POSH has been used to categorise these follow-up activities. Name them, and then discuss what will be involved in each case.

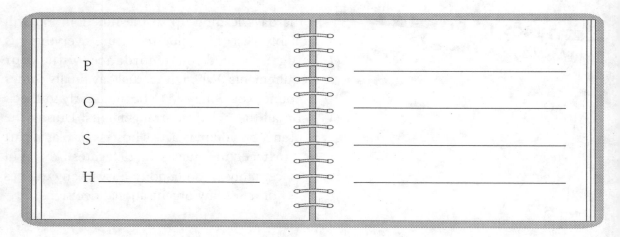

P _____ _____

O _____ _____

S _____ _____

H _____ _____

Videoconferencing

If it is not possible for people from distant locations to meet at a common location, videoconferencing is ideal. Confravision is a service provided by British Telecom in the UK which uses sound and vision to hold meetings. BT Confravision studios are located in many major cities and participants go to any of these studios to operate a videoconferencing link with participants in other cities. Links with different countries are also possible using satellite.

Videostream is another service provided by BT. It enables videoconferencing to take place in ordinary offices using a television camera and monitor.

Using either of these methods the only time taken is the actual meeting time itself. There is no excessive preparations or lengthy travelling time and there will be considerable savings on expenses which would otherwise be incurred with hotels, etc.

Obviously videoconferencing is expensive, but there are many benefits to be gained. Can you think of some?

_____   _____

_____   _____

Quick Quiz

Conferences

1   List the three major items which require preliminary decisions before proceeding with conference planning.

_____   _____

_____   _____

2   When booking a venue list three items which should be confirmed in a covering letter apart from the day and date of the conference.

_____   _____

_____   _____

3   When contacting potential speakers, name three items of information you must give them apart from the day and date of the conference.

_____   _____

_____   _____

4   When speakers have accepted your invitation, name two things you must obtain from them as soon as possible.

_____

_____

5   Suggest three items of equipment which might be necessary at a conference.

_____   _____

_____   _____

6　What special requirements must be considered when choosing menus or refreshments?

_____

_____

7　Name four checks you will need to make on the day of the conference.

_____　　_____

_____　　_____

8　How will you find out the reactions of delegates to the conference?

_____

_____

9　What follow-up will be necessary after the conference?

_____

_____

10　Suggest three advantages of videoconferencing.

_____　　_____

_____　　_____

Review

1　You work for the Sales and Marketing Director of Turner Communications. Your employer has called a meeting with the six Regional Sales Managers to discuss the launch of a new range of mobile communication equipment. Suggest a variety of visual aids and documentation which will be required.

5.3 TRAVEL ARRANGEMENTS

Some larger companies have a special department dealing with travel arrangements for all company staff. However, very often making arrangements for executive travel is another main aspect of the secretary's role. Business trips could be taken within your own country or overseas, and your employer may travel for many reasons. They are:

You forgot this!

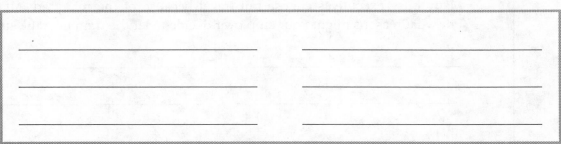

A systematic approach to preparing for a trip is essential. The various actions to be taken are illustrated in this flowchart.

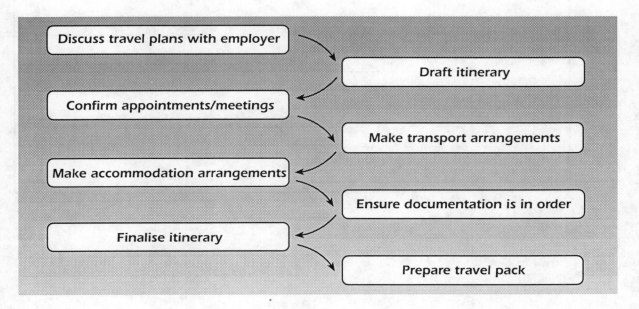

Transport Arrangements

Many travel agents offer efficient services in suggesting appropriate travel and making the necessary reservations. Finding a good agent and maintaining a good relationship with them will relieve you of much of the stress involved in organising travel.

1   *Road transport*

   If your employer wishes to take his/her own car overseas, certain requirements must be considered. List some of them below.

   _____   _____

   _____   _____

2   *Rail travel*

   Many busy executives choose rail travel because of the many advantages. For what reasons might your employer decide to let the train take the strain?

   _____   _____

   _____   _____

3   *Air travel*

   Your regular travel agent will be able to advise about any special offers available and when details have been agreed they will prepare the tickets for you. When planning air travel, what considerations must be taken into account?

   _____   _____

   _____   _____

   _____   _____

Appointments and Meetings

Some functions may already have been confirmed but you may have to plan other appointments and meetings for your employer. When planning such appointments do remember certain considerations:

_____   _____

_____   _____

_____   _____

After making your appointments, you will need to send out letters or faxes to confirm them.

Accommodation Arrangements

If your employer has visited a region before, he/she may have preferences regarding hotels. Otherwise special handbooks and tourist guides are available or your travel agent will be pleased to make recommendations. Your employer must be consulted regarding single/double room requirements and any special dietary concerns. Letters confirming arrangements must include several important details:

_____   _____

_____   _____

_____   _____

Documentation

The documentation required for a business trip will depend on the regions/countries to be visited. The documentation which may be necessary is illustrated in this mnemonic. Complete each item and discuss the requirements under each heading. Make separate notes for your files as you discuss each item.

P_____

L_____

T_____

C_____

H_____

Itinerary

Once all details are finalised, an itinerary must be prepared. This will be an essential reference document for your employer during his trip. You will also need a copy in case you need to contact your employer. Other colleagues or superiors may also need to know your employer's movements.

 You will no doubt be familiar with itineraries from Transcription lessons. However, it will be useful to discuss format and content. Type out a copy of an itinerary to post on your classroom wall.

Travel Pack

You must ensure that your employer is thoroughly prepared for all eventualities during his/her trip. Discuss the material which your employer may need to take with him/her.

The Employer's Absence

Your employer's absence is not an excuse to take it easy. You should ensure that work continues to run smoothly while your employer is away, dealing with all contingencies calmly and efficiently.

How will you deal with the following?

Mail _____

_____

_____

Telephone Calls _____

_____

_____

Keeping yourself busy _____

_____

_____

_____

_____

How will you prepare for your employer's return?

_____

_____

_____

_____

_____

_____

_____

Quick Quiz

Travel Arrangements

Answer these questions.

1   In an initial telephone call to your travel agent regarding a proposed overseas trip for your employer, suggest three pieces of information you must provide.

_____

_____

_____

2   When confirming accommodation requirements by fax, name what three important details which must be included?

_____

_____

3   What is the name of the document which shows the traveller's movements during his/her trip?

_____

4   Who will you contact to find out if a Visa is required for travel to a particular country?

_____

5   Suggest two methods which your employer could use to pay for goods/services while overseas?

_____

_____

6   Apart from passport/visa/itinerary, name two important documents which might be necessary for an overseas trip.

_____

_____

7   Suggest four essential items which your employer should take on an overseas trip.

_____   _____

_____   _____

8   How will you deal with your employer's mail during his/her absence?

_____

_____

9   Suggest two things you could do during your employer's absence.

_____

_____

10   Suggest some preparations you would make for your employer's return to the office?

_____

_____

_____

_____

Review

1   Your employer has been invited to Hong Kong to attend a Business Exhibition. He intends to stay for three nights and wishes to meet some clients while he is there.

   a   What travel arrangements will need to be made?
   b   What other arrangements will be necessary?

2   Prepare an itinerary for the visit mentioned in question 1. Your employer will travel on a Monday morning and return on Thursday afternoon. The Business Exhibition is at the Mandarin Towers Hotel on Tuesday afternoon from 1400 to 1630, with an official dinner at 1830. Make up any other necessary details.

5.4 SOURCES OF INFORMATION

A lot of responsibility falls on the shoulders of the secretary, but she cannot be expected to remember everything. What is essential is that you are organised in such a way that you can find information when it is needed, or know who to contact or ask.

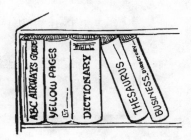

Several general reference sources may be used daily by a secretary. List them.

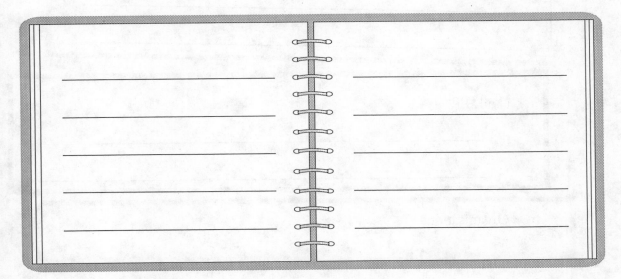

Check it out! You may also find it useful to subscribe to journals and magazines dealing with office equipment or the secretarial function. Which periodicals in your country would be useful?

Other essential sources of reference will depend on the nature of your job as well as their availability. In what reference books would you find information regarding the following?

1   Road Travel

2 Rail Travel

_____

_____

3 Air Travel

_____

_____

4 People

_____

_____

5 Organisations

_____

_____

External Reference Agencies

Information which you need may not always be available in printed form. A lot of advice and information can be obtained by making a telephone call, but of course you need to know who to call. There are a variety of information services, national bodies, specialised bureaux or local service agencies. Such organisations exist to provide help with a variety of matters such as local business activity, help with staff recruitment, delivery of urgent documents or even obtaining tickets for an exhibition.

What sort of external agencies are available in your area?

_____   _____

_____   _____

_____   _____

Computerised Information Services (Videotex)

A great deal of information is now stored in computers. Information can be accessed using a telecommunications link and specially adapted television receiver or VDU. There are two forms of videotex.

1   *Teletext*

Teletext is the name given to databases provided by television companies which supply general information on various topics such as weather conditions, travel, currency exchange rates, holiday destinations, stock market. In the UK there are two public teletext services - Oracle from the BBC and Ceefax from ITV.

2   *Viewdata*

In the UK a public viewdata service called Prestel is operated by British Telecom and accessed via the telephone system. A user's VDU is connected with databases of information provided by various organisations and updated regularly. Prestel is a two-way service so users can both receive and send information. This is useful for placing orders, authorising transfers from banks and making hotel reservations.

Check it out!   Does your country have Teletext or Viewdata systems? How do they work?

Quick Quiz

Sources of Information

A   *In which reference book would you find information about the following?*

1   The correct spelling of a word   _____

2   John Lennon   _____

3   Paul McCartney   _____

4   Flights from Tokyo to Toronto   _____

5   A major company in the UK   _____

6   Details of postal services
and current rates   _____

7   A synonym for a word which
your employer has used twice
in one sentence   _____

8   Telephone numbers of
electricians in your area   _____

9   The population of a foreign country   _____

10   The location of a hotel in Tokyo   _____

B   *Suggest which external agencies you might contact for information or help with the following.*

1   Mortgage advice   _____

2   Local business activity   _____

3   Accountancy and tax advice   _____

4   Printing and presentation of reports   _____

5   Improving the company's image
or promoting a new product   _____

6   Recruitment of senior staff   _____

7   Industrial relations and
employment legislation   _____

8   Information about entry and
regulations in a foreign country   _____

9   Financial details of a
registered company   _____

| 10 | Reserving tickets to see Pavarotti, who is appearing in your city in three months' time | _____ |

Review

1 a Suggest four sources of reference which would be useful for a receptionist.

 b List two items of information which you could obtain from the following.

 i Travel agent
 ii Post Office Guide
 iii Yellow Pages
 iv Business card

2 Suggest three external reference sources which a secretary may use in the course of her work. Give reasons.

The Secretary in Practice

6.1 PERSONAL WORK PLANNING

'Fail to plan and you plan to fail.' A familiar expression but very true. Although it may be tempting to put aside your least favourite task in preference for something which you enjoy, it may not always be practical.

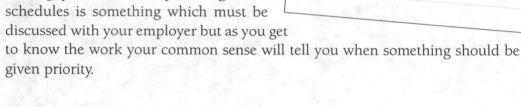

Most jobs will include some aspects of work which occurs at regular intervals, eg on a daily, weekly, monthly or quarterly basis. It will be helpful to identify these patterns so that work can be planned efficiently.

Setting priorities and planning work schedules is something which must be discussed with your employer but as you get to know the work your common sense will tell you when something should be given priority.

Your Workstation

Organising your desk and immediate workstation is probably the first step in cultivating efficient working practices. Apart from a typewriter, computer or word processor, list the items you will need at your workstation or even on the office walls around you.

Organising yourself and your environment is an important first step, and from there it should be possible to deal with work priorities in an orderly manner. A useful practice every evening is to write a list of things to be done on the following day. When you arrive at work you can then work through the list systematically. This planned and organised approach will help you feel in control and cope with any contingencies.

Diaries

In order to help plan ahead, your office diary will be essential. You will also look after your employer's diary and perhaps also monitor his pocket diary.

DIARY

2 October
Monday

Morning 1000 New temp – Margaret

Afternoon 1400 Rep to service fax

Evening 1800 Mum's for dinner

DIARY

3 October
Monday

Morning 0830 Mr. G's anniversary
(send flowers to wife)

Afternoon 1230 Lunch with new guy
from sales!

Evening 1900 Hyatt Hotel Lobby
Meet Joe

Your employer's diary will record business meetings and other important items such as:

_____

_____

_____

_____

Your diary will be more comprehensive, keeping a note of your employer's commitments and other things such as:

_____

_____

_____

_____

Considerations to be taken into account in managing office diaries are as follows.

1   Always _____ with the employer before confirming any appointment.

2   Provisional engagements should be entered in _____ so that it is easy to see which are actually confirmed.

3   Every _____, discuss the day's appointments with your employer and prepare any necessary files and papers for the appointments. Use this opportunity also to update each other on any other entries.

4   Avoid scheduling _____ appointments after a lengthy meeting or late in the day.

5   Allow time in case appointments _____.

6   Keep your employer's activities _____ when liaising with others to plan further commitments.

7   Take good care of the diary and take note of the _____ for each appointment. If your employer is running late you could telephone visitors about potential delays.

 **Check it out!** Do you have any tips from your own experience in dealing with office diaries?

Electronic Diaries

Computerisation means you can keep details of all appointments on an electronic diary. Diary pages can be scanned according to page, week, month or year and can keep up to five years' records. Holiday time can be blocked out, memory joggers inserted, priority tasks highlighted, cross references made to appropriate text. Details of meetings can be transmitted to electronic diaries of others involved in a meeting and if someone is not available this will be indicated. A search can then be made for a suitable time and date for all members.

 Discuss the advantages and disadvantages of the electronic diary system. Make notes for your file.

Visual Control Boards

One useful aid to planning and controlling your activities is to use a visual control board. These boards show the whole year at a glance and can be updated or revised quickly. Coloured markers, codes or adhesive strips may be used to indicate different activities.

When would these visual control boards be particularly useful?

_____

_____

_____

Reminder Systems

Follow-up, reminder, tickler or bring forward systems. Different names for the same thing - a memory jogger. Such a system is essential to highlight items which need your attention or your employer's at the appropriate time.

 Suggest a suitable procedure which you could use as a bring forward system. Make notes for your file.

Daily Routines

It is useful to develop a routine with your employer particularly at the beginning and end of each day. Below are some examples of the daily routines of a secretary.

Beginning of the day

- Open mail and sort

- Check incoming faxes and e-mail

- Attach relevant documents or files

- Check voicemail messages

- Check reminder system

- Take mail, follow-up papers and diary into employer's office

- Discuss the day's appointments and receive instructions regarding transcription of correspondence

Routine activities

- Check today's action list

- Continue with work

- Deal with dictation or instructions from employer as necessary

- Screen employer's calls and put through or take messages as necessary

- Receive visitors and show them in to employer as necessary

- Receive faxes/e-mail and deal appropriately

- Do any filing as necessary

At end of morning/afternoon

- Take in correspondence for signature when convenient

- Consult employer regarding following day's appointments

- Update action checklist

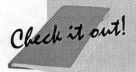

Director of Turner Communications returns to the office next Monday after a two week business trip which included a four day conference. His secretary has arranged the following appointments for the day of his return. Discuss this schedule and make comments.

0930   Donald Andrews, a customer complaining about faulty goods

1000   Meeting with Managing Director who wishes to know your opinion about the conference and details of new contacts

1200   Lunch with Mr Len Dayton from Inter-Links plc at Mandarin Hotel (possible new client)

1330   Monthly meeting with Sales Representatives in your office

1630   Helen Jordan, Counter Assistant, wishes to see you on a personal matter

Review

1   How would you use an electronic diary to schedule internal meetings?

2   You work for the Company Secretary and one of her responsibilities is to ensure renewal of all the company's many insurances. What method could you use to ensure that your employer does not forget to renew them at the appropriate time?

3   Today's in-tray includes the following items for your employer. State the action you would take regarding each item.

a   A letter for your employer marked 'Personal'.
b   An internal memo regarding a meeting to be held next month.
c   A fax from your travel agent giving provisional flights and dates for your employer's trip to Europe in three weeks' time and asking for confirmation.
d   An invitation to a major supplier's annual dinner which your employer normally attends.
e   A letter from a former employee asking for a testimonial.

Communication is one of the most important aspects of the secretary's role. She spends her entire day communicating in some form or another - talking on the telephone or face-to-face with a person, transcribing business correspondence, receiving and giving instructions, liaising with colleagues or staff of different hierachical levels and also with business contacts.

As the majority of a secretary's time is actually spent communicating with people verbally, it is essential to develop an appropriate, efficient and courteous manner in all forms of oral communications, whether with people within or outside the office.

Below are some situations you will have to deal with.

Internally

- answer telephone calls
- take messages
- participate in meetings
- liaise with employer's superiors/peers
- correct damaging gossip
- handle unhelpful colleagues
- handle complaining customers
- resolve office conflicts

Externally

- receive callers
- handle unwelcome callers
- research information
- act as hostess at special functions
- deal with the press
- resolve problem situations

The consequences of poor communication could be disastrous. For example, discuss what might happen in these situations.

Internally, a message was communicated inappropriately or inaccurately.

_____

_____

Externally, a situation was handled badly or the wrong information was communicated in the wrong manner.

_____

_____

Protocol

In dealing with people and situations the secretary can do a lot to enhance or discredit the image of both the employer and the company. What is needed is a constant awareness of communicating appropriately while retaining courtesy at all times. It will take time to build up a reputation for professionalism and efficiency, but constant attention to this vital aspect will pay dividends in the long-term.

How would you define protocol?

_____

_____

_____

The Secretary and Communication

Special qualities are required for dealing with people with whom you may come into contact during the course of your work. These different people are illustrated in the following diagram. Write some adjectives beneath each heading which describe your manner and behaviour in dealing with the people in each category.

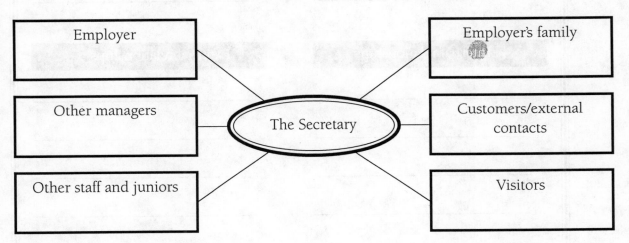

Creating a Good Impression

Learning how to deal appropriately with people is a skill which will be developed. The important thing to remember is that you are in effect a public relations officer for your employer and your organisation, both internally and externally. In an increasingly competitive world you must aim to create and maintain a good impression.

Discuss how you can ensure that you give a good impression in each of the following categories.

Presentation of work	Presentation of yourself

Internal relationships	External relationships

Review

1   You are secretary to the Personnel Director who is in a meeting with the Personnel Manager and an employee who is accepting voluntary redundancy. They have asked not to be disturbed. How would you deal with the following situations?

    a   A business acquaintance calls to arrange a meeting with your employer. He wants to discuss whether your company will require a stand at a forthcoming education and training exhibition.

    b   The Security Officer calls to talk with your employer about a matter he says is quite urgent.

    c   The Managing Director's secretary calls to ask your employer to attend an urgent meeting with the MD immediately.

    d   A member of the press calls to ask if rumours regarding redundancies are true.

2   You work for the Purchasing Manager of an estate agency and your employer is overseas until early next week. How would you deal with the following situations?

    a   A client calls to make an offer for an important property. When you try to put the call through to the Negotiation Manager there is no reply.

    b   An invoice is received from a regular supplier totalling £50,000. You believe this is quite a lot more than the quotation originally received.

    c   A supplier calls to say they wish to send an urgent quotation by fax but are unable to communicate via your departmental fax machine.

What is a Secretary?

The word 'secretary' means different things to different people. In one company a secretary may be someone who opens the mail, answers the phone, transcribes correspondence, makes tea and runs errands. In another company a secretary may be a personal assistant providing a full support service to a senior executive.

As roles differ so much, there can be no exact definition, but each secretary's role will be unique according to various factors. Write them below.

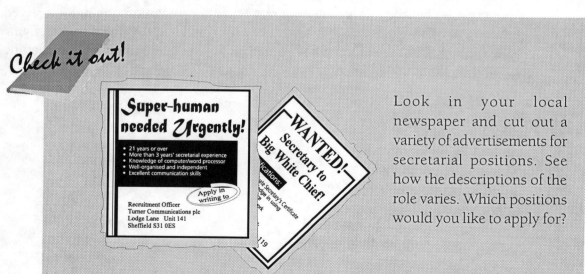

Check it out!

Look in your local newspaper and cut out a variety of advertisements for secretarial positions. See how the descriptions of the role varies. Which positions would you like to apply for?

Professional Journals and Associations

When you qualify as a secretary and develop your secretarial expertise in practice, it may be worthwhile subscribing to a professional magazine and joining an association which recognises your professional status. Are there such magazines and organisations in your area? Make a list in the chart below.

Journals	Organisations

Discuss the benefits which you would gain by regular subscription to these magazines or by joining a professional association.

Further Qualifications

As you gain experience you may decide to take further courses to achieve higher qualifications, perhaps so that you can advance to a different position in your own company or elsewhere.

What qualifications might you consider studying for in the future?

_____

_____

_____

_____

_____

Certificate

This is to Certify that _Iris Tan Siew May_

has successfully completed a one-year Advanced Secretarial Course which included the following subjects:

Communication - Use of English   Secretarial Administration

Audio Transcription   Management Appreciation

Manuscript Transcription   Meetings and Minute-taking

Ms Sally Turner
Principal

Mr Douglas Allen
Managing Director

Review

1   Suggest some ways in which you could prepare yourself for advancement in your career.

2   The post of Head of Secretarial Services at a new branch of your company is being advertised. Responsibilities will include setting up office systems, purchasing office furniture and materials, recruiting and training junior staff. Discuss the work experience and personal qualities you would expect from the person appointed.

Appendix

Examination Papers

No. **PR-OP 11**
30097

CANDIDATE'S NAME ....

(Block letters please)

CENTRE NO. ....DATE ....

TIME ALLOWED: TWO HOURS
(plus 10 minutes' reading time).

You are advised to read Part 2 carefully during the reading time.

PART 1   Answer ALL questions in Section A and Section B. Your answers should be written on the sheets provided. You are advised to spend no more than 1 hour on this part.

PART 2   Answer ALL questions in Section A and any TWO from Section B.

Ensure that your name is written clearly at the top of each of your sheets.

When you have finished the examination your answers to Part 2 should be firmly attached to this question paper.

FOR EXAMINER'S USE ONLY

PART 1 A	B	PART 2 A	B1	B2	B3	TOTAL
20	30	20	15	15	15	100

PART 1

Section A

Complete each of the following 2p sentences by filling in the missing word or phrase in the space provided. (1 mark each)

1   A document which should be securely locked in an office is: ....

2   .... is a television service which allows business executives to have face-to-face discussions when they are in different countries.

3   FIFO (First In First Out) is a method used to issue .... in an office.

4   Before binding a set of documents, a/an .... may be used to make sure the edges of the papers are even.

5   A/an .... must be used with numerical filing.

6   A/an .... is a **written** communication from one department of a company to another.

7   Analysis columns are used in a/an .... Book.

8   Vertical, lateral, rotary are all examples of filing ....

9   .... is the allowance made by a wholesaler to a retailer.

10   For safety, a/an .... should be fitted to the blade of a guillotine.

11   Because she is not working from **written** text, a/an ..../typist should be good at spelling and punctuation.

12   .... are filed in specially-large cabinets, with shallow drawers.

13   "Enc" written at the bottom of a business letter means ....

14   In order to keep confidentiality, a/an .... may have to be keyed in before using a computer.

15   A/an .... is used to record injuries which happen at work.

16   A/an .... is sent to the customer when he has been undercharged on an invoice.

17   In a/an .... index, information details are written on one line.

18   Incoming letters marked .... must be dealt with immediately.

19   A new disk must be .... before the disk drive will read it.

20   The mail room clerk may use .... to sort the mail into different departments.

(Total 20 marks)

Section B

Answer each of the following 10 questions BRIEFLY in the spaces provided. (3 marks each)

1   State three day to day procedures for operating a filing system.

     a)   ....

     b)   ....

     c)   ....

2   Which office staff in a large company would be responsible for the following tasks?

     a)   Receiving visitors ....

     b)   Using the franking machine ....

     c)   Storing and retrieving documents ....

3   Name **three** advantages of telephone compared with fax.

     a)   ....

     b)   ....

     c)   ....

4   Give **three** reasons why back-up disks are made.

     a)   ....

     b)   ....

     c)   ....

5   **Three** methods of producing copies of documents are:

     a)   ....

     b)   ....

     c)   ....

6   Put the following three business documents into correct sequence of the order in which they are prepared:

     a)   Invoice   b)   Order   c)   Quotation

     1   ....

     2   ....

     3   ....

7   Which filing classifications would be most suitable for the following?

    a)   A travel agent ....

    b)   A solicitor ....

    c)   A garage vehicle parts department ....

8   What do the following terms found on a stationery stock card indicate?

    a)   Receipts ....

    b)   Issues ....

    c)   Balance ....

9   Three **written** kinds of business communication are:

    a)   ....

    b)   ....

    c)   ....

10   List **three** common causes of accidents in the office.

    a)   ....

    b)   ....

    c)   ....

(Total 30 marks)

PART 2

Section A - COMPULSORY question. (20 marks)

Assume you are employed by Timepieces Ltd and are responsible for writing invoices and seeing to the distribution of various copies within the firm. You have just received the Order below from County Jewellers Ltd.

County Jewellers Ltd
100 High Street, Newton N14 4RD

ORDER NO: 331   Tel: 3792 248921
                                           Fax: 3792 448921

DATE: (Yesterday's date)

Timepieces Ltd
Century Works
Bridgeway
19 6HY

Please supply:

Cat No	Quantity	Description	Price each £
6-A70	8	Ladies Fun Watch - enamelled case	30.00
6-A75	4	Ladies Fashion Watch - gold plate case with black roman numerals	40.00
6-A82	4	Ladies Quality Watch - gold plated case - jewelled movement	100.00

DELIVERY: **Immediate**

Signed *A B Someton*
For County Jewellers Ltd

Complete the invoice form on page 7 using today's date.

(Total 20 marks)

PART 2 (continued)

Section B

Answer any TWO of the following questions. (15 marks each)

1   A printout of a school database is shown below:

SURNAME	FORENAME	FORM	STUDENT NO
Davis	Paul	5A2	500
Smithe	Angela	5B2	507
McDonald	Judy	5A3	508
Van Dam	Ruth	5B1	509
Farmerton	Peter	5A4	513
Smith	Paul	5B2	515
Farmer	Gladys	5A2	529
Davies	Derek	5A1	537
Vandenburg	David	5B3	539
MacDonald	Rosemary	5B2	551

i)   Which filing classification has been used?   (1 mark)

ii)   Write out all the names again, this time arranging them in strict alphabetical order.
                                                                      (5 marks)

iii)   Give **two** reasons why you think the school has not used alphabetical order for its
       pupils   (2 marks)

iv)   Draw an absent card to be used in place of Gladys Farmer's file.   (7 marks)
                                                                      (Total 15 marks)

2   Describe the following services and in each case name a situation in which it would be
      used.

      a)   Telephone conference call.   (5 marks)
      b)   Transferred charge call or collect call.   (5 marks)
      c)   Emergency service.   (5 marks)
                                                                      (Total 15 marks)

3   Your firm is considering buying a new copier.

      Write a memo: (3 marks)

             a)   listing the features which you think the new machine should have;
                                                                      (6 marks)

             b)   describing **two** systems which the firm could use to record the
                    amount of copying done by each department.   (6 marks)
                                                                      (Total 15 marks)

TIMEPIECES LTD
Century Works
Bridgeway
19 6HY

INVOICE NO: 7171

Tel: 012-339-5161
Fax: 012-33-7171

ORDER NO:
ORDER DATE:

DATE:

TO:

Terms: 3% for monthly settlement

Quantity	Description	Cat No	Item Price £	Total Price £

TOTAL goods		
LESS: 10% Trade Discount		
NEW TOTAL		
TOTAL Government Tax 15%		
TOTAL BALANCE DUE		

END OF EXAMINATION

OFFICE PROCEDURES

LEVEL 2

No. **PR–OP 12**
20158

PITMAN
EXAMINATIONS
INSTITUTE

PAST PAPER

CANDIDATE'S NAME ....
(Block letters please)

CENTRE NO. ....DATE ....

TIME ALLOWED: 2 hours 30 minutes
                  (plus 10 minutes' reading time).

PART 1:   All questions should be attempted. The relevant
                 forms included in this paper should be used.
                 The information required to answer these questions
                 is given in the Scenario. You are advised to spend not
                 more than 60 minutes on this part.

PART 2:   Answer any <u>THREE</u> questions.

Ensure that your name is written clearly at the top of each of your answer sheets.

Use diagrams or sketches wherever you feel they help your answer.

Calculators may be used.

FOR EXAMINER'S USE ONLY

PART 1	PART 2			TOTAL
40	20	20	20	100

1992   J/IA/LFN

SCENARIO

The following details will be needed in both parts of the paper:

The tasks are based at SALTER SNACKS LTD, a firm manufacturing crisps, salted nuts, savoury biscuits and other snack foods.

The head office and factory are at Washington Business Park, Western Road, Exeter, Devon EX42 3HN

```
                        Board of Directors
                         |
                        Managing Director
                         |
    ┌──────────┬─────────┴──────────┬────────────────┐
Works Manager  Sales Manager    Accountant      Personnel Manager
(Joan Trott)   (Tony Baker)     (Colin Cross)   (Mary Banks)
```

The office hours are 0900 to 1730, with lunch from 1230-1330. The offices are not currently staffed during the lunch period.

You work for Sarah Patel, Assistant Sales Manager, but in times of holidays or sickness you help out as required.

Sarah's car has a 1300 cc engine and qualifies for a mileage allowance of 32 pence per mile.

One of the organisations that you trade with is

Orpington Social Club   Telephone 081 433566
48-52 Castle Street
Orpington
Kent
DA32 4KB

PART 1 *(40 marks)*

Answer ALL questions.

Documents required in connection with these tasks are given on pages 4-7.

1   Sarah Patel has handed you a page from her diary showing her expenses for the week
        commencing Monday 29th. Work out her car mileage and complete the expense claim
        form.   *(14 marks)*

2   You are just going to lunch when you receive a telephone call from John Smith of Orpington
        Social Club. The latest batch of packets of salted cashew nuts are not of the usual quality.
        The outer boxes appear to have had something spilled on them, and he says that there
        were similar problems with the last batch. He would like Sarah to ring back as soon as
        possible (after 1600 hours as he will be out of the office until then). Sarah is in a meeting
        but will be back shortly. Fill in the message form.   *(5 marks)*

3   Valley Restaurant has telephoned to complain that Invoice No E409/91 is incorrect.

        a)   Please check the invoice, circle any entries that are incorrect and put the correct
                entry alongside.   *(4 marks)*

        b)   Write a letter of apology to the company, which you will fax today, acknowledging
                the error and explaining how it will be rectified.

                                                                                (7 marks)

4   You have seen a job advertisement and are interested in applying. On enquiry you are told
        that an application form will not be supplied; applicants are asked to write in giving full
        details.

        a)   Why does a firm require a written application?

                                                                                (2 marks)

        b)   What type of documents would you submit as your application.

                                                                                (2 marks)

        c)   List the sort of information that you would supply.

                                                                                (6 marks)
                                                                          (Total 40 marks)

_____

DATA FOR PART 1

BIRMINGHAM												
85	BRISTOL											
107	45	CARDIFF										
157	81	120	EXETER									
55	53	58	126	HEREFORD								
98	178	200	250	116	LIVERPOOL							
63	74	109	152	80	165	OXFORD						
199	125	164	45	168	294	193	PLYMOUTH					
112	52	98	91	102	217	62	134	SALISBURY				
87	179	202	249	148	76	143	293	205	SHEFFIELD			
128	75	122	108	128	237	65	149	23	205	SOUTHAMPTON		
126	48	87	32	95	220	121	75	67	221	89	TWYFORD	
117	119	155	170	135	210	56	215	82	167	78	167	LONDON

Appointments	Expenses	Appointments	Expenses
29 Monday 2pm Weston Products – visit new site at Twyford	Mileage?	9am Interviews at Head Office – all day	**2 Friday**
30 Tuesday 9am Head Office 1pm – Coates Ltd at Salisbury Discuss new range – Lunch Overnight	Lunch £60 Mileage? Hotel £90		**3 Saturday**
31 Wednesday Drive to Southampton – Brown & Co On to Universal Products at Oxford Overnight	Mileage? Mileage? Hotel £62		**4 Sunday**
1 Thursday 12 noon – Hoe Products at Plymouth 1pm Lunch Return to Head Office	Mileage? Lunch £52 Mileage?		

FORM FOR USE IN PART 1

Candidate's Name ....

CLAIM FOR EXPENSES

Claimant's Name _____

Department _____

Date	Particulars of Travel	Car Engine cc	Rail/ Air*	Hotel Acc'dtn*	Meals*	Others* eg Taxis	Daily Totals
		£	£	£	£	£	£
	Total mileage _____ miles @ _____ per mile						
	* Bills and receipts should be attached Please specify other expenses overleaf						
Authorised and Checked by					Grand Total	£	

Date _____

MESSAGE FOR

M _____

WHILE YOU WERE OUT

M _____

Of _____

Telephone No _____

Telephoned		Please ring	
Called to see you		Will call again	
Wants to see you		Urgent	

Message: _____

_____

_____

_____

_____

_____

_____

_____

Date _____ Time _____

Received by _____

```
INVOICE                                                        No E409/91

                    S A L T E R   S N A C K S   L T D
                        Washington Business Park
                             Western Road
                               Exeter
                               Devon
                              EX42 3HN

Telephone 071 223322
Fax       071 111222

To    Valley Restaurant
      The Square
      Reigate
      Surrey RH42 1PQ                     Date    xx xxxxxxx 199x
```

Quantity	Description	Cat No	Unit Price £	Cost £
90 pkts	Salted peanuts	K122	0.22	198.00
60 pkts	Cashew nuts	K133	0.32	19.20
12 boxes	Salt & Vinegar crisps	P134	2.50	30.00
10 jars	Stuffed olives	S101	1.40	14.00
				333.20
				24.99
				309.21

```
Less 7.5% trade discount
```

PART 2 (20 marks each)

Answer any THREE of the following questions:

1   The safety record of your company has deteriorated with a resultant increase in absence.

   a)   The Personnel Manager asks you to draft a memo reminding employees of their responsibilities in respect of safety.

(7 marks)

   b)   Describe 4 actions that can be taken to improve safety in the office, indicating what types of accident would be prevented.

(8 marks)

   c)   Describe 5 ways of avoiding the problems associated with working with VDUs.

(5 marks)
(Total 20 marks)

2   a)   Prepare a notice of meeting and an agenda for a meeting of the Canteen Committee to be held in Committee Room A on the first Monday of next month at 1000 hours. As well as the usual items include:

Price Increases
Introduction of New Dishes
Opening Times

(8 marks)

   b)   Explain what you understand by the following:

      i)   Quorum
      ii)   Ad hoc
      iii)   Point of Order

(6 marks)

   c)   Prepare a checklist of 6 tasks that you would perform on the day of the meeting in preparing the room.

(6 marks)
(Total 20 marks)

3   You are asked to be responsible for the reception area during the absence of the full-time receptionist.

a)   Explain the duties that might be performed by the receptionist in taking responsibility for the security of the reception area. Give examples where appropriate.

(5 marks)

b)   Explain the advantages of a telephone answering machine to Salter Snacks. Describe the features available that might assist Sarah when her work takes her away from the office.

(5 marks)

c)   Prepare a message to be recorded on the telephone answering machine.

(4 marks)

d)   You overhear the following conversation. Make constructive comments.

Receptionist *Hello*

Caller *Is that Salter Snacks Ltd?*

Receptionist *Yes it is*

Caller *Can I speak to Tony Brown please?*

Receptionist *He's not in today*

Caller *It is rather urgent*

Receptionist *Could you ring back tomorrow?*

Caller *Well I'm only in this country for a few days and I wanted to talk about purchasing some of your products.*

Receptionist *I could try the Assistant Sales Manager for you.*

Caller *Thank you*

Receptionist *(After a few minutes) She's not in her office either. Why don't you ring her this afternoon?*

(6 marks)
(Total 20 marks)

4   Some documents cannot be found in the filing system. Draft a report to the Office Manager in which you:

a)   identify **4** likely reasons for this failure.

(8 marks)

b)   describe ways in which these problems can be avoided.

(10 marks)

c)   recommend appropriate action.

(2 marks)
(Total 20 marks)

5   Your company is planning a sales drive which will include a personalised mail shot to all customers drawing attention to the new products.

     a)   Suggest the most appropriate way of producing a 3 page letter. Justify your suggestions.

                                                       (8 marks)

     b)   Describe how your supportive literature might be prepared.

                                                       (9 marks)

     c)   Select the 6 items that would be helpful to the mailroom in sending off this mailshot.

                                                       (3 marks)

                                                    (Total 20 marks)

END OF EXAMINATION

**ADMINISTRATION AND SECRETARIAL
PROCEDURES**

LEVEL 3

No.   **PR–ASP 13
30134**

PITMAN
EXAMINATIONS
INSTITUTE

PAST PAPER

CANDIDATE'S NAME ....
(Block letters please)

CENTRE NO. ....DATE ....

TIME ALLOWED: THREE HOURS
plus 10 minutes' reading time.

PART 1   Answer all questions.

PART 2   Answer any <u>THREE</u> questions.

*Ensure that your name is written clearly at the top of each of your
answer sheets.*

Use diagrams or sketches wherever you feel they help your answer.

FOR EXAMINER'S USE ONLY

PART 1	PART 2			TOTAL
40	20	20	20	100

Sir Isaac Pitman Ltd   1993

K/IB/LFC

SCENARIO

The following information will be needed in Part 1 of the paper:

You are employed as Personal Assistant to John Cochrane, Company Secretary of Newall Engineering Ltd, Civil Engineers, whose Head Office is in London. It is an international company with branch offices in many parts of the world. The policy of the company is that, apart from chief engineers and top management, the selection and employment of personnel is dealt with on a local basis.

In the case of Head Office, the Company Secretary is responsible for all matters relating to office staff, their recruitment and health and safety. As the company has just obtained a contract to build a bridge in Wales, it plans to employ sufficient staff to see the contract through to its successful conclusion.

You provide full secretarial support to your employer, assist him in all matters relating to the recruitment and induction of office staff and are responsible for the supervision of office juniors.

PART 1

Mr Cochrane is in Wales today. When you arrive at the office the following THREE tasks form part of your work:

Task 1

a)   Draft an Application Form   *(7 marks)*

b)   Draft a letter   *(6 marks)*

Task 2

a)   Prepare a Job Description.   *(8 marks)*

b)   Draw up a checklist for an Induction Programme.   *(7 marks)*

Task 3

a)   Check and amend Minutes.   *(7 marks)*

b)   Draft the Agenda.   *(5 marks)*

Please complete them using the details provided.

(Total 40 marks)

Task 1

PA/

Now that we have the new contract for the bridge we shall have to recruit new staff!

Please design a job application form asking the usual questions – So that I can look at it when I get back. Please also draft a letter which can be sent to all successful applicants, inviting them for interview. Leave blanks for items that will need to be inserted later – you know the sort of things I mean, dates, etc.

JC

Task 2

PA/

The new contract will generate a lot of work for you so you will need additional help.

Prepare a Job Description for a junior shorthand-typist so that you can delegate some of your secretarial work.

It may be a little while before there are sufficient new staff to arrange a full induction programme, so I should like you to provide a preliminary session for the new office staff. Please cover all the usual topics. Make a checklist of these and we can discuss it on my return.

JC

Task 3   Candidate's Name ....

SAFETY COMMITTEE MEETING MINUTES

A meeting was held in the Board Room of the Safety Committee.

Present

Mrs I Butler
B Hickson
S Maharajah
Miss J Baruc
J Cochrane (in the chair)

Apologies	None
Minutes	Minutes of last month's meeting agreed and signed by Mr Cochrane.
Matters Arising	None
Fire	Mr Hickson said that not all of the staff knew about our policy for reporting a fire. Miss Baruc said that this should be in the Staff Handbook. Mrs Butler said we needed safety notices. They agreed that the Staff Handbook would be discussed at next month's meeting and that arrangements for the design of safety notices would be made by mrs Butler.
First Aid	Everyone agreed with Mr Maharajah's idea that Mr Cochrane organise a course for first aiders, on the lines discussed at the last meeting.
Any other business	Miss Baruc raised the question of whether the Accident Book could be kept in a more accessible place. The committee decided to think about this and talk about it at the next meeting.
Date of next meeting	In the Board Room at 2.30 in exactly 4 weeks from today.

The junior typist who serviced the safety committe meeting last Thursday at 2·30 pm in your absence has given me these minutes. Please check them, neatly cross through any errors and write in your corrections on the minutes so she can have them back to re-type.

Also, would you please prepare the Agenda for the next meeting – only one new item – "Health and Safety Policy"

Thanks JC

NB ATTACH THIS PAGE TO YOUR ANSWER SHEETS.

Intentionally Blank

PART 2

Answer any THREE questions.

Each question carries 20 marks.

1   The control and monitoring of the financial records of a business are important for security purposes and for the most effective use of resources.

    a)   Explain the importance of reconciling bank statements, giving reasons why errors and discrepancies may occur.   *(9 marks)*

    b)   Draw up a set of security rules for the safe handling of cash in the office.   *(5 marks)*

    c)   State SIX factors that are important when choosing the means of payment when travelling abroad.   *(6 marks)*
    (Total 20 marks)

2   Effective communication is essential to the success of an organisation.

    a)   Identify and discuss TEN factors which affect the choice of external communications.   *(10 marks)*

    b)   What is electronic mail? Explain how it can operate internally and externally in an organisation.   *(10 marks)*
    (Total 20 marks)

3   a)   Explain TWO factors that influence the ways in which organisations are structured and explain why such structures are often expressed in terms of charts and diagrams.   *(7 marks)*

    b)   Define line, staff and functional relationships in an organisation and the secretary's role within them.   *(13 marks)*
    (Total 20 marks)

4   The organisation for which you work is considering the introduction of a computerised system of information and records management.

    a)   Explain any problems that may be encountered in transferring to and operating a computerised record system and suggest how these may be overcome.   *(10 marks)*

    b)   Compare the advantages and disadvantages of computerised filing.   *(10 marks)*
    (Total 20 marks)

END OF EXAMINATION

SERIES 4 EXAMINATION 1995

OFFICE PROCEDURES

SECOND LEVEL

(Code No: 2027)

THURSDAY 30 NOVEMBER 1995

LONDON CHAMBER *of* **COMMERCE & INDUSTRY**

COMMERCIAL EDUCATION TRUST

EXAMINATIONS BOARD

Instructions to Candidates

*(a)   The time allowed for this examination is **2** hours.*

*(b)   Answer **5** questions.*

(c)   All questions carry equal marks.

(d)   Put a line through any rough work.

(e)   The use of standard English dictionaries and cordless non-programmable calculators is permitted.   Candidates whose first language is not English may use a bilingual dictionary.

(f)   Write legibly and pay particular attention to clarity of expression, spelling, punctuation and layout.

*(g)   **Secretarial Studies Certificate***

   (i)   This examination is a compulsory component of the Secretarial Studies Certificate award.

   (ii)   When taken as an SSC component in the United Kingdom, the examination should be scheduled from 0930 to 1130.

The candidate works for Comlon International plc, Comlon House, West Street, London SW1Y 2AR.

1 (a) What is the function of the O & M Department?

   (b) What are the essentials of good systems or procedures?

2 Comlon International plc sends several thousand circulars to a regular mailing list of customers twice a month. Describe **4** specific items of mail room equipment which would help in this work.

3 (a) The following documents are used in the process of buying and selling. Describe the purpose of each document:

        (i)   internal requisition
        (ii)   quotation
        (iii) invoice

                                                                              (15 marks)

   (b) Value Added Tax is mentioned on some of these documents. Explain what VAT is.
                                                                              (5 marks)

4 (a) Describe **4** different types of computer printer.
                                                                              (12 marks)

   (b) What factors would you consider when choosing a printer?
                                                                              (8 marks)

5 (a) Why is it necessary for an organisation to retain information?
                                                                              (4 marks)

   (b) What are the advantages and disadvantages of using microfilm in this connection?
                                                                              (16 marks)

6 (a) What is meant by a flexitime system?

   (b) What are the advantages and disadvantages to both the employer and the employee of using flexitime?

7 What steps would you take to try to ensure your use of the telephone was as cost-effective as possible?

8 (a) List the items which lead to inefficient use of time in an office.
                                                                              (8 marks)

   (b) How can time be better managed?
                                                                              (12 marks)

9   (a)   Describe **4** of the following telephone facilities:

  (i)   conference call
  (ii)   Imtran
  (iii) call barring
  (iv)   call logging
  (v)   abbreviated dialling

(12 marks)

  (b)   What are the advantages to Comlon International plc in using these?

(8 marks)

10 (a)   Describe **3** types of wall board which would be useful at a conference centre.

(12 marks)

  (b)   Suggest the types of information you would expect to be displayed.

(8 marks)

SERIES 4 EXAMINATION 1995

OFFICE ORGANISATION AND SECRETARIAL PROCEDURES

THIRD LEVEL

(Code No: 3305)

THURSDAY 7 DECEMBER 1995

_____

Instructions to Candidates

(a) The time allowed for this examination is **2** hours **30** minutes.

(b) Answer **5** questions.

(c) All questions carry equal marks.

(d) Put a line through any rough work.

(e) The use of standard English dictionaries and cordless non-programmable calculators is permitted. Candidates whose first language is not English may use a bilingual dictionary.

(f) Write legibly and pay particular attention to clarity of expression, spelling, punctuation and layout.

(g) **Private Secretary's Certificate**

(i) This examination is a compulsory component of the Private Secretary's Certificate award.

(ii) When taken as a PSC component in the United Kingdom, the examination should be scheduled from 0930 to 1200.

The candidate works for Comlon International plc, Comlon House, West Street, London SW1Y 2AR.

1 As a secretary how would you ensure that information is not disclosed to any unauthorised person?

2 Identify the various documents used in buying and selling and explain the function and use of **3** of the documents.

3 Describe, with suggestions for appropriate use, **5** methods of internal communication within an organisation.

4 Details of a new product have been leaked to the press.

    (a) Suggest ways of dealing with the present situation.

                  (6 marks)

    (b) What action should be taken to prevent a recurrence?

                  (14 marks)

5 At the monthly departmental meeting your manager will make a presentation to the sales staff about a new product which will be launched shortly.

    (a) What arrangements would you have to make prior to the meeting?

    (b) What audio/visual aids might be needed to assist with the presentation?

6 You have just had an integrated WP/Spreadsheet/Database package installed on your computer. Explain how you might make use of **each** of these facilities in your role as secretary to the Office Services Manager.

7 Explain, with examples, **4** of the following terms:

    (a) incentive schemes
    (b) equal opportunities
    (c) disciplinary procedures
    (d) bonus schemes
    (e) flexible working hours
    (f) fringe benefits

8 (a) Explain the purposes served by an efficient stock control system.

    (b) List the procedures to be followed for the efficient issue of stock.

9 What are the methods by which a company may promote itself?

10 Secretarial agencies can be very useful when recruiting temporary staff.

    (a) Identify the benefits to your organisation of using an agency.

                  (12 marks)

    (b) What factors would you take into consideration when selecting the agency to use?

                  (8 marks)

Index